Practice Behaviors Workbook

Introduction to Social Work and Social Welfare

ELEVENTH EDITION

Charles Zastrow
George Williams College of Aurora University

Prepared by

Vicki Vogel
University of Wisconsin, Whitewater

Australia • Brazil • Japan • Korea • Mexico • Singapore • Spain • United Kingdom • United States

BROOKS/COLE
CENGAGE Learning

© 2014 Brooks/Cole, Cengage Learning

ALL RIGHTS RESERVED. No part of this work covered by the copyright herein may be reproduced, transmitted, stored, or used in any form or by any means graphic, electronic, or mechanical, including but not limited to photocopying, recording, scanning, digitizing, taping, Web distribution, information networks, or information storage and retrieval systems, except as permitted under Section 107 or 108 of the 1976 United States Copyright Act, without the prior written permission of the publisher.

For product information and technology assistance, contact us at
**Cengage Learning Customer & Sales Support,
1-800-354-9706**

For permission to use material from this text or product, submit all requests online at **www.cengage.com/permissions**
Further permissions questions can be emailed to
permissionrequest@cengage.com

ISBN-13: 978-1-285-17648-2
ISBN-10: 1-285-17648-0

Brooks/Cole
20 Davis Drive
Belmont, CA 94002-3098
USA

Cengage Learning is a leading provider of customized learning solutions with office locations around the globe, including Singapore, the United Kingdom, Australia, Mexico, Brazil, and Japan. Locate your local office at:
www.cengage.com/global

Cengage Learning products are represented in Canada by Nelson Education, Ltd.

To learn more about Brooks/Cole, visit
www.cengage.com/brookscole

Purchase any of our products at your local college store or at our preferred online store
www.cengagebrain.com

Printed in the United States of America
1 2 3 4 5   19 18 17 16 15

Contents

Chapter		Page
Contents		iii
Introduction		iv
Chapter 1:	Social Welfare: Its Business, History, and Future	1
Chapter 2:	Social Work as a Profession and a Career	8
Chapter 3:	Generalist Social Work Practice	16
Chapter 4:	Poverty and Public Welfare	23
Chapter 5:	Emotional/Behavioral Problems and Counseling	30
Chapter 6:	Family Problems and Services to Families	36
Chapter 7:	Sexual Orientation and Services to GLBT Individuals	46
Chapter 8:	Drug Abuse and Drug Treatment Programs	52
Chapter 9:	Crime, Juvenile Delinquency, and Correctional Services	58
Chapter 10:	Problems in Education and School Social Work	65
Chapter 11:	Work-Related Problems and Social Work in the Workplace	71
Chapter 12:	Racism, Ethnocentrism, and Strategies for Advancing Social And Economic Justice	77
Chapter 13:	Sexism and Efforts for Achieving Equality	85
Chapter 14:	Aging and Gerontological Services	95
Chapter 15:	Health Problems and Medical Social Services	105
Chapter 16:	Physical and Mental Disabilities and Rehabilitation	112
Chapter 17:	Overpopulation, Misuse of the Environment, and Family Planning	117

NOTE TO INSTRUCTORS:
Commentary to instructors is located in the Instructors Manual and includes information/ answers for some of the exercises found in this workbook.

Empowerment Series

Dear Social Work Student,

Welcome to *Competencies/Practice Behaviors Workbook* for Zastrow's *Introduction to Social Work and Social Welfare*, 11e. Throughout your course you will acquire a great deal of new knowledge, including an introduction to new theories, informative research, and practical skills like critical thinking skills and frameworks for appreciating and overcoming challenges. All of the knowledge you gain will offer you a deeper, richer understanding of social work. Used in conjunction with your text and other resources, the *Competencies/Practice Behaviors Workbook* presents you with Practice Exercises that will teach you how to transform your new knowledge into social work Practice Behaviors.

About Competence and Practice Behaviors

In social work, the words Competence and Practice Behavior have a unique meaning beyond the typical dictionary definitions. "Competence" in the usual sense means that a person possesses suitable skills and abilities to do a specific task. A competent baseball player must move quickly, catch, throw, and play as part of a team. They also have to think quickly, understand the rules of the game, and be knowledgeable of their environment. In the same way, a competent social worker should be able to do a number of job-related duties, think critically, and understand the context of their work. The Council on Social Work Education (CSWE) has defined specific Core Competency areas for all social work students, and their corresponding Practice Behaviors as follows:

Competencies and Practice Behaviors
2.1.1: Identify as a Professional Social Worker and Conduct Oneself Accordingly
a. Advocate for client access to the services of social work
b. Practice personal reflection and self-correction to assure continual professional development
c. Attend to professional roles and boundaries
d. Demonstrate professional demeanor in behavior, appearance, and communication
e. Engage in career-long learning
f. Use supervision and consultation
2.1.2: Apply Social Work Ethical Principles to Guide Professional Practice
a. Recognize and manage personal values in a way that allows professional values to guide practice
b. Make ethical decisions by applying standards of the National Association of Social Workers Code of Ethics and, as applicable, of the International Federation of Social Workers/ International Association of Schools of Social Work Ethics in Social Work, Statement of Principles
c. Tolerate ambiguity in resolving ethical conflicts
d. Apply strategies of ethical reasoning to arrive at principled decisions

2.1.3: Apply Critical Thinking to Inform and Communicate Professional Judgments

a. Distinguish, appraise, and integrate multiple sources of knowledge, including research-based knowledge and practice wisdom
b. Analyze models of assessment, prevention, intervention, and evaluation
c. Demonstrate effective oral and written communication in working with individuals, families, groups, organizations, communities, and colleagues

2.1.4: Engage Diversity and Difference in Practice

a. Recognize the extent to which a culture's structures and values may oppress, marginalize, alienate, or create or enhance privilege and power
b. Gain sufficient self-awareness to eliminate the influence of personal biases and values in working with diverse groups
c. Recognize and communicate their understanding of the importance of difference in shaping life experiences
d. View themselves as learners and engage those with whom they work as informants

2.1.5: Advance Human Rights and Social and Economic Justice

a. Understand the forms and mechanisms of oppression and discrimination
b. Advocate for human rights and social and economic justice
c. Engage in practices that advance social and economic justice

2.1.6: Engage in Research-Informed Practice and Practice-Informed Research

a. Use practice experience to inform scientific inquiry
b. Use research evidence to inform practice

2.1.7: Apply Knowledge of Human Behavior and the Social Environment

a. Utilize conceptual frameworks to guide the processes of assessment, intervention, and evaluation
b. Critique and apply knowledge to understand person and environment

2.1.8: Engage in Policy Practice to Advance Social and Economic Well-Being and to Deliver Effective Social Work Services

a. Analyze, formulate, and advocate for policies that advance social well-being
b. Collaborate with colleagues and clients for effective policy action

2.1.9: Respond to Contexts that Shape Practice

a. Continuously discover, appraise, and attend to changing locales, populations, scientific and technological developments, and emerging societal trends to provide relevant services
b. Provide leadership in promoting sustainable changes in service delivery and practice to improve the quality of social services

2.1.10: Engage, Assess, Intervene, and Evaluate with Individuals, Families, Groups, Organizations and Communities

a. Substantively and affectively prepare for action with individuals, families, groups, organizations, and communities
b. Use empathy and other interpersonal skills
c. Develop a mutually agreed-on focus of work and desired outcomes
d. Collect, organize, and interpret client data
e. Assess client strengths and limitations
f. Develop mutually agreed-on intervention goals and objectives
g. Select appropriate intervention strategies
h. Initiate actions to achieve organizational goals
i. Implement prevention interventions that enhance client capacities

j.	Help clients resolve problems
k.	Negotiate, mediate, and advocate for clients
l.	Facilitate transitions and endings
m.	Critically analyze, monitor, and evaluate interventions

Each of the Exercises in the *Competencies/Practice Behaviors Workbook* will focus on learning and applying social work Practice Behaviors. While every Exercise will not ask you to apply Competencies or Practice Behaviors from every Core Competency area, by the time you finish your course you will have practiced many and gained a better working knowledge of how social work is done. The goal, shared by your professors, your program, the authors of this text, and by Brooks/Cole, Cengage Learning Social Work team, is that by the end of your curriculum you will have honed your Practice Behaviors in all of the Core Competency areas into a skill set that empowers you to work effectively as a professional social worker.

Assessing Competence: Partnering with Your Instructor and Peer Evaluator
As described above, the Council on Social Work Education clearly defines the Competencies and Practice Behaviors that a social work student should be trained to employ. Therefore, the grading rubric that comes at the end of every chapter of the *Competencies/Practice Behaviors Workbook* is adapted from Competencies and Practice Behaviors defined by CSWE (see the table above). To assess your competence during your course, we recommend you partner with a peer(s) who can act as your course "evaluator(s)" to genuinely assess both your written assignments and your role-plays; be sure to ask your professor to comment on and approve the assessments once they are completed by you and your Evaluator. It is our hope that partnering with your classmates in this way will familiarize you with the unique learning opportunity you will have in your Field Experience – the signature pedagogy of social work education. There you will apply all of your knowledge and skills under the supervision of your Field Instructor and Field Liaison before completing your required curriculum.

As always, we thank you for your commitment to education and to the profession. Enjoy your course, and *feel empowered to help others*!

Chapter 1: Social Welfare: Its Business, History, and Future

Competencies/Practice Behaviors Exercise 1.1
Ice Breaker: Getting Acquainted

Focus Competencies or Practice Behaviors:
- EP 2.1.1b   Practice personal reflection and self-correction to assure continual professional development

A. Brief Description
    This exercise is designed to help you become acquainted with one another and to provide the instructor with information as to what you want to learn from the class.

B. Objectives
    You will:
    1. Become acquainted with one another.
    2. Specify information you wish to learn from the class.
    3. Ask the instructor questions about his or her own work experiences in social work.

C. Procedure
    1. You will be seated in a circle, and each of you will be asked to provide the following information:
        a. Name
        b. Why you are taking the course
        c. One or two things you want to learn from the course
        d. The event that, to date, has had the greatest impact on your life

    2. What would you like to know about your instructor, such as paid work experiences in social work, special interests in social work, and teaching experience? Your instructor will endeavor to answer all questions (except those of a private, personal nature).

Competencies/Practice Behaviors Exercise 1.2
Ice Breaker: Searching for Descriptors

Focus Competencies or Practice Behaviors:
- EP 2.1.1b   Practice personal reflection and self-correction to assure continual professional development

A. Brief Description
    This exercise is designed to facilitate interaction among you and to begin to create a positive class atmosphere.

B. Objectives
    You will
    1. Become more acquainted with your classmates.
    2. Practice interviewing skills.

C. Procedure
1. The instructor will pass out a list of descriptors on a sheet of paper to each student. (A descriptor is a word or phrase that identifies an item.) Some possibilities are listed below. Each of you will need to find one student (or two or three students in larger classes) who says "yes" to having specific descriptors. (Each student can only be listed once on the sheet by each "searcher.") After several minutes the instructor will indicate that the time is up. The instructor will then read each descriptor, and ask for the names of those who were listed by at least one "searcher."

Sample Descriptors

1. Plays golf
2. Likes classical music
3. Is a fan of the Dallas Cowboys
4. Has had a paid or volunteer job related to social work
5. Was born west of the Mississippi River
6. Has traveled in Mexico
7. Is married
8. Likes to jog
9. Has never flown on an airplane
10. Has meditated
11. Has water-skied
12. Has been to a gay pride festival
13. Has traveled in Canada
14. Has gone deer hunting
15. Enjoys fishing
16. Attends church regularly
17. Has received a speeding ticket
18. Has visited, or lived on, a reservation
19. Played a varsity sport in high school
20. Has heard of Jane Addams who founded Hull House in Chicago

Competencies/Practice Behaviors Exercise 1.3
Blaming the Victim

Focus Competencies or Practice Behaviors:
- EP 2.1.4a   Recognize the extent to which a culture's structures and values may oppress, marginalize, alienate, or create or enhance privilege and power
- EP 2.1.5a   Understand forms and mechanisms of oppression and discrimination

A. Brief Description
The purpose of this exercise is to demonstrate that in our society people who are victimized are often blamed for their misfortunes and predicaments.

B. Objectives
You will:
1. Identify people who have been victimized and then blamed for their misfortunes.
2. Refute the statements provided below.

C. Procedure
1. Following are examples to illustrate that people who are victimized are often blamed for their predicaments:
   a. A rape victim is erroneously said to have dressed or behaved in such a way as to entice the rapist.
   b. A woman who is battered by her husband is erroneously accused of inviting the battering by being "bitchy." (It is interesting to note that males in our society are seldom referred to as "bitchy.")
   c. Mothers who are receiving public assistance are often erroneously stereotyped as promiscuous, irresponsible, and having little motivation to work outside the home.

2. Identify ways in which people who are victimized in our society are often blamed for their misfortunes and predicaments.

3. Write a report refuting the statements. Research articles and studies regarding these statements, and cite your references.

Competencies/Practice Behaviors Exercise 1.4
Surrogate Motherhood and Cloning

Focus Competencies or Practice Behaviors:
- EP 2.1.1b Practice personal reflection and self-correction to assure continual professional development
- EP 2.1.2a Recognize and manage personal values in a way that allows professional values to guide practice

A. Brief Description
   The purpose of this exercise is to have you assess the merits and shortcomings of the advance in reproductive technology—namely, surrogate motherhood.

B. Objectives
   You will:
   1. Explore your personal feelings about this surrogate motherhood.

C. Procedure
   1. It is possible for a woman to become a genetic mother of a child without having sexual intercourse and without being pregnant. Test-tube fertilization and the embryo transfer technique make this possible. This technique is available, even though there is considerable debate regarding whether this reproductive technology is desirable.

   2. List the merits and shortcomings of this approach, and state whether you feel this technology is desirable or undesirable.

Competencies/Practice Behaviors Exercise 1.5
Role Play—The Tea Party Movement—Is This the Rebirth of Social Darwinism?

Focus Competencies or Practice Behaviors:
- EP 2.1.1b   Practice personal reflection and self-correction to assure continual professional development
- EP 2.1.1c   Attend to professional roles and boundaries
- EP 2.1.1d   Demonstrate professional demeanor in behavior, appearance, and communication
- EP 2.1.2a   Recognize and manage personal values in a way that allows professional values to guide practice
- EP 2.1.3a   Distinguish, appraise, and integrate multiple sources of knowledge, including research-based knowledge and practice wisdom
- EP 2.1.3c   Demonstrate effective oral and written communication in working with individuals, families, groups, organizations, communities, and colleagues
- EP 2.1.4a   Recognize the extent to which a culture's structures and values may oppress, marginalize, alienate, or create or enhance privilege and power
- EP 2.1.10b   Use empathy and other interpersonal skills

A. Brief Description
   This role play is designed to explore your own thoughts about the tea party movement and revisit the concept of Social Darwinism.

B. Objectives
   You will:
   1. Be able to debate the pros and cons of the tea party movement and social Darwinism.
   2. Practice role playing controversial topics while respecting differing points of view.

C. Procedure
   1. Review the material in the chapter regarding the tea party movement and the rebirth of social Darwinism.
   2. Form two groups, with one or two classmates in each group—one group in agreement with the concepts involved and the other in opposition.
   3. Role play a vigorous debate for approximately 15 minutes.
   4. Discuss the difficulties involved with understanding and respecting points of view that differ from your own personal beliefs.

Chapter 1 Competencies/Practice Behaviors Exercises Assessment:

Name: _____ Date: _____

Supervisor's Name: _____

Focus Competencies/Practice Behaviors:
- EP 2.1.1b   Practice personal reflection and self-correction to assure continual professional development
- EP 2.1.1c   Attend to professional roles and boundaries
- EP 2.1.1d   Demonstrate professional demeanor in behavior, appearance, and communication
- EP 2.1.2a   Recognize and manage personal values in a way that allows professional values to guide practice
- EP 2.1.3a   Distinguish, appraise, and integrate multiple sources of knowledge, including research-based knowledge and practice wisdom
- EP 2.1.3c   Demonstrate effective oral and written communication in working with individuals, families, groups, organizations, communities, and colleagues
- EP 2.1.4a   Recognize the extent to which a culture's structures and values may oppress, marginalize, alienate, or create or enhance privilege and power
- EP 2.1.5a   Understand forms and mechanisms of oppression and discrimination
- EP 2.1.10b   Use empathy and other interpersonal skills

Instructions:
A. Evaluate your work or your partner's work in the Focus Competencies/Practice Behaviors by completing the Competencies/Practice Behaviors Assessment form below
B. What other Competencies/Practice Behaviors did you use to complete these Exercises? Be sure to record them in your assessments

1.	I have attained this competency/practice behavior (in the range of 81 to 100%)
2.	I have largely attained this competency/practice behavior (in the range of 61 to 80%)
3.	I have partially attained this competency/practice behavior (in the range of 41 to 60%)
4.	I have made a little progress in attaining this competency/practice behavior (in the range of 21 to 40%)
5.	I have made almost no progress in attaining this competency/practice behavior (in the range of 0 to 20%)

EPAS 2008 Core Competencies & Core Practice Behaviors	Student Self Assessment						Evaluator Feedback
Student and Evaluator Assessment Scale and Comments	0	1	2	3	4	5	Agree/Disagree/Comments
EP 2.1.1 Identify as a Professional Social Worker and Conduct Oneself Accordingly:							
a. Advocate for client access to the services of social work							
b. Practice personal reflection and self-correction to assure continual professional development							
c. Attend to professional roles and boundaries							
d. Demonstrate professional demeanor in behavior, appearance, and communication							
e. Engage in career-long learning							
f. Use supervision and consultation							

EP 2.1.2 Apply Social Work Ethical Principles to Guide Professional Practice:						
a.	Recognize and manage personal values in a way that allows professional values to guide practice					
b.	Make ethical decisions by applying NASW Code of Ethics and, as applicable, of the IFSW/IASSW Ethics in Social Work, Statement of Principles					
c.	Tolerate ambiguity in resolving ethical conflicts					
d.	Apply strategies of ethical reasoning to arrive at principled decisions					
EP 2.1.3 Apply Critical Thinking to Inform and Communicate Professional Judgments:						
a.	Distinguish, appraise, and integrate multiple sources of knowledge, including research-based knowledge and practice wisdom					
b.	Analyze models of assessment, prevention, intervention, and evaluation					
c.	Demonstrate effective oral and written communication in working with individuals, families, groups, organizations, communities, and colleagues					
EP 2.1.4 Engage Diversity and Difference in Practice:						
a.	Recognize the extent to which a culture's structures and values may oppress, marginalize, alienate, or create or enhance privilege and power					
b.	Gain sufficient self-awareness to eliminate the influence of personal biases and values in working with diverse groups					
c.	Recognize and communicate their understanding of the importance of difference in shaping life experiences					
d.	View themselves as learners and engage those with whom they work as informants					
EP 2.1.5 Advance Human Rights and Social and Economic Justice:						
a.	Understand forms and mechanisms of oppression and discrimination					
b.	Advocate for human rights and social and economic justice					
c.	Engage in practices that advance social and economic justice					
EP 2.1.6 Engage in Research-Informed Practice and Practice-Informed Research:						
a.	Use practice experience to inform scientific inquiry					
b.	Use research evidence to inform practice					
EP 2.1.7 Apply Knowledge of Human Behavior and the Social Environment:						
a.	Utilize conceptual frameworks to guide the processes of assessment, intervention, and evaluation					
b.	Critique and apply knowledge to understand person and environment					
EP 2.1.8 Engage in Policy Practice to Advance Social and Economic Well-Being and to Deliver Effective Social Work Services:						
a.	Analyze, formulate, and advocate for policies that advance social well-being					

b.	Collaborate with colleagues and clients for effective policy action						
EP 2.1.9 Respond to Contexts that Shape Practice:							
a.	Continuously discover, appraise, and attend to changing locales, populations, scientific and technological developments, and emerging societal trends to provide relevant services						
b.	Provide leadership in promoting sustainable changes in service delivery and practice to improve the quality of social services						

EP 2.1.10 Engage, Assess, Intervene, and Evaluate with Individuals, Families, Groups, Organizations and Communities:							
a.	Substantively and affectively prepare for action with individuals, families, groups, organizations, and communities						
b.	Use empathy and other interpersonal skills						
c.	Develop a mutually agreed-on focus of work and desired outcomes						
d.	Collect, organize, and interpret client data						
e.	Assess client strengths and limitations						
f.	Develop mutually agreed-on intervention goals and objectives						
g.	Select appropriate intervention strategies						
h.	Initiate actions to achieve organizational goals						
i.	Implement prevention interventions that enhance client capacities						
j.	Help clients resolve problems						
k.	Negotiate, mediate, and advocate for clients						
l.	Facilitate transitions and endings						
m.	Critically analyze, monitor, and evaluate interventions						

Chapter 2: Social Work as a Profession and a Career

Competencies/Practice Behaviors Exercise 2.1
Forming an Identity

Focus Competencies or Practice Behaviors:
- EP 2.1.1b   Practice personal reflection and self-correction to assure continual professional development
- EP 2.1.1e   Engage in career-long learning
- EP 2.1.2a   Recognize and manage personal values in a way that allows professional values to guide practice

A. Brief Description
This exercise provides a questionnaire to help in identity formation.

B. Objectives
You will:
1. Be provided with information to help you form a sense of who you are.
2. Examine the extent to which you have already formulated a personal identity.
3. Identify specific areas you have to focus on in order to formulate a more thorough sense of who you are.

C. Procedure
1. Read the following questionnaire, and write your answers to the questions.
2. If this exercise is shared with the class, this questionnaire will remain confidential, and you will not be asked to identify yourself.

Questionnaire
Arriving at a Sense of Who I am and What I Want out of Life

1. What do I find satisfying/meaningful/enjoyable? (Only after you identify what is meaningful and gratifying will you be able to consciously seek involvement in activities that will make your life fulfilling and avoid those activities that are meaningless or stifling.)

2. What is my moral code? (One possible code is to seek to fulfill your needs and to seek to do what you find enjoyable, doing so in a way that does not deprive others of the ability to fulfill their needs.)

3. What are my religious beliefs?

4. What kind of a career do I desire? (Ideally, you should seek a career in which you find the work stimulating and satisfying, that you are skilled at, and that earns you enough money to support the lifestyle you want.)

5. What are my sexual mores? (All of us should develop a consistent code that we are comfortable with and that helps us to meet our needs without exploiting others. There is no one right code—what works for one may not work for another, due to differences in lifestyles, life goals, and personal values.)

6. Do I desire to marry? (If yes, to what type of person and when? How consistent are your answers here with your other life goals?) If you are married, is marriage overall fulfilling for you, and do you want to remain married?

7. Do I desire to have children? (If yes, how many and when? How consistent are your answers here with your other life goals?) If you have children, do you want to have more children?

8. What area of the country/world do I desire to live in? (Variables to be considered are climate, geography, type of dwelling, rural or urban setting, closeness to relatives or friends, and characteristics of the neighborhood.)

9. What do I enjoy doing with my leisure time?

10. What kind of image do I want to project to others? (Your image will be composed of your dressing style and grooming habits, your emotions, personality, degree of assertiveness, capacity to communicate, material possessions, moral code, physical features, and voice patterns. You need to assess your strengths and shortcomings honestly in this area, and seek to make improvements.)

11. What type of people do I enjoy being with and why?

12. Do I desire to improve the quality of my life and that of others? (If yes, in what ways? How do you hope to achieve these goals?)

13. What types of relationships do I desire to have with relatives, friends, neighbors, with people I meet for the first time?

14. What are my thoughts about death and dying?

15. What are currently the most severe stresses in my life?

16. How am I handling these stresses? What strategies am I using to resolve them?

17. What do I want to accomplish in the next five years?

18. What are my plans for accomplishing the goals I listed in question 17?

Competencies/Practice Behaviors Exercise 2.2
Suspended from High School

Focus Competencies or Practice Behaviors:
- EP 2.1.1b   Practice personal reflection and self-correction to assure continual professional development
- EP 2.1.1e   Engage in career-long learning
- EP 2.1.2a   Recognize and manage personal values in a way that allows professional values to guide practice
- EP 2.1.3a   Distinguish, appraise, and integrate multiple sources of knowledge, including research-based knowledge and practice wisdom
- EP 2.1.3b   Analyze models of assessment, prevention, intervention, and evaluation
- EP 2.1.3c   Demonstrate effective oral and written communication in working with individuals, families, groups, organizations, communities, and colleagues

A. Brief Description
You will learn how to use the problem-solving approach in a group.

B. Objectives
You will:
1. Learn the problem-solving approach and apply this approach to a situation.
2. Apply critical thinking to provide reasons for your answers to the questions provided after this exercise.

C. Procedure
1. The stages of the problem-solving approach are as follows:
   a. Identifying and defining the problem
   b. Assessing the size and causes of the problem
   c. Developing alternative strategies or plans for solving it
   d. Assessing the merits and shortcomings of these alternative strategies
   e. Selecting and implementing the most desirable strategy or strategies
   f. Evaluating the success of the strategies used

2. Apply the problem-solving approach to the following situation:

> Five students have been suspended for a four-day period for drinking alcoholic beverages at their high school, which is located in a small city of 5,400. It has been the policy of the school board to suspend any student who has been caught drinking alcoholic beverages at school. In the past five months a total of 16 students have been suspended. The police department is unhappy with the suspensions because when the students are suspended they usually loiter on the city streets during school hours. The school social worker contacted the parents of the five suspended students, and only one couple indicated an interest in receiving counseling for their daughter. The other parents stated that they weren't sufficiently concerned to talk further about the suspension.

3. Answer the following five questions:
   a. What do you see as being the most serious problem to deal with?
   b. What do you believe are the causes of this problem?
   c. What possible strategies could you follow to combat this problem?
   d. What do you see as the merits and shortcomings of each of these strategies?
   e. Which of these strategies would you select to combat the problem you have identified?
4. State the reasons for your answers.

Competencies/Practice Behaviors Exercise 2.3
Role Play—A Home Visit with a Hostile Client

Focus Competencies or Practice Behaviors:
- EP 2.1.1b   Practice personal reflection and self-correction to assure continual professional development
- EP 2.1.1d   Demonstrate professional demeanor in behavior, appearance, and communication
- EP 2.1.3c   Demonstrate effective oral and written communication in working with individuals, families, groups, organizations, communities, and colleagues
- EP 2.1.4a   Recognize the extent to which a culture's structures and values may oppress, marginalize, alienate, or create or enhance privilege and power
- EP 2.1.10a   Substantively and affectively prepare for action with individuals, families, groups, organizations, and communities
- EP 2.1.10j   Help clients resolve problems

A. Brief Description
   This role play is designed to mentally prepare social workers in possible confrontations with clients.

B. Objectives
   You will:
   1. Be able to experience hostile situations in a controlled environment.
   2. Practice professional demeanor.

C. Procedure
   1. Read the following vignette.
   2. Divide the class into pairs. Each person in the pair will role play the social worker as well as the client.
   3. One person will perform the client role in the vignette—keep it clean and safe, while the other person performs the social worker role.
   4. The students in each pair will then switch roles and perform the vignette their own way.
   5. In each role play, the social worker will exhibit professional skills and portray the safety skills suggested in the chapter.

> Sylvester has had a history of drug abuse, mainly with meth. There have been many 911 calls from Sylvester's wife, Tallulah, to this home. She has had numerous broken bones and black eyes, yet she refuses to leave him. She says that when he is not using meth, he is a "sweetheart."
>
> The social worker has made an appointment for a home visit. You will begin the role play as the social worker knocks on the door and Sylvester slams open the door and yells, "What the hell do you want?"

6. Discuss whether the social worker in each situation portrayed the safety skills discussed in the chapter, including de-escalation techniques, as well as front-end preparation.

Chapter 2 Competencies/Practice Behaviors Exercises Assessment:

Name: _____ Date: _____
Supervisor's Name: _____

Focus Competencies/Practice Behaviors:
- EP 2.1.1b   Practice personal reflection and self-correction to assure continual professional development
- EP 2.1.1d   Demonstrate professional demeanor in behavior, appearance, and communication
- EP 2.1.1e   Engage in career-long learning
- EP 2.1.2a   Recognize and manage personal values in a way that allows professional values to guide practice
- EP 2.1.3a   Distinguish, appraise, and integrate multiple sources of knowledge, including research-based knowledge and practice wisdom
- EP 2.1.3b   Analyze models of assessment, prevention, intervention, and evaluation
- EP 2.1.3c   Demonstrate effective oral and written communication in working with individuals, families, groups, organizations, communities, and colleagues
- EP 2.1.4a   Recognize the extent to which a culture's structures and values may oppress, marginalize, alienate, or create or enhance privilege and power
- EP 2.1.10a   Substantively and affectively prepare for action with individuals, families, groups, organizations, and communities
- EP 2.1.10j   Help clients resolve problems

Instructions:
A.   Evaluate your work or your partner's work in the Focus Competencies/Practice Behaviors by completing the Competencies/Practice Behaviors Assessment form below
B.   What other Competencies/Practice Behaviors did you use to complete these Exercises? Be sure to record them in your assessments

1.	I have attained this competency/practice behavior (in the range of 81 to 100%)
2.	I have largely attained this competency/practice behavior (in the range of 61 to 80%)
3.	I have partially attained this competency/practice behavior (in the range of 41 to 60%)
4.	I have made a little progress in attaining this competency/practice behavior (in the range of 21 to 40%)
5.	I have made almost no progress in attaining this competency/practice behavior (in the range of 0 to 20%)

EPAS 2008 Core Competencies & Core Practice Behaviors	Student Self Assessment						Evaluator Feedback
Student and Evaluator Assessment Scale and Comments	0	1	2	3	4	5	Agree/Disagree/Comments
EP 2.1.1 Identify as a Professional Social Worker and Conduct Oneself Accordingly:							
a. Advocate for client access to the services of social work							
b. Practice personal reflection and self-correction to assure continual professional development							
c. Attend to professional roles and boundaries							
d. Demonstrate professional demeanor in behavior, appearance, and communication							
e. Engage in career-long learning							
f. Use supervision and consultation							

EP 2.1.2 Apply Social Work Ethical Principles to Guide Professional Practice:							
a.	Recognize and manage personal values in a way that allows professional values to guide practice						
b.	Make ethical decisions by applying NASW Code of Ethics and, as applicable, of the IFSW/IASSW Ethics in Social Work, Statement of Principles						
c.	Tolerate ambiguity in resolving ethical conflicts						
d.	Apply strategies of ethical reasoning to arrive at principled decisions						
EP 2.1.3 Apply Critical Thinking to Inform and Communicate Professional Judgments:							
a.	Distinguish, appraise, and integrate multiple sources of knowledge, including research-based knowledge and practice wisdom						
b.	Analyze models of assessment, prevention, intervention, and evaluation						
c.	Demonstrate effective oral and written communication in working with individuals, families, groups, organizations, communities, and colleagues						
EP 2.1.4 Engage Diversity and Difference in Practice:							
a.	Recognize the extent to which a culture's structures and values may oppress, marginalize, alienate, or create or enhance privilege and power						
b.	Gain sufficient self-awareness to eliminate the influence of personal biases and values in working with diverse groups						
c.	Recognize and communicate their understanding of the importance of difference in shaping life experiences						
d.	View themselves as learners and engage those with whom they work as informants						
EP 2.1.5 Advance Human Rights and Social and Economic Justice:							
a.	Understand forms and mechanisms of oppression and discrimination						
b.	Advocate for human rights and social and economic justice						
c.	Engage in practices that advance social and economic justice						
EP 2.1.6 Engage in Research-Informed Practice and Practice-Informed Research:							
a.	Use practice experience to inform scientific inquiry						
b.	Use research evidence to inform practice						
EP 2.1.7 Apply Knowledge of Human Behavior and the Social Environment:							
a.	Utilize conceptual frameworks to guide the processes of assessment, intervention, and evaluation						
b.	Critique and apply knowledge to understand person and environment						
EP 2.1.8 Engage in Policy Practice to Advance Social and Economic Well-Being and to Deliver Effective Social Work Services:							
a.	Analyze, formulate, and advocate for policies that advance social well-being						
b.	Collaborate with colleagues and clients for effective policy action						

EP 2.1.9 Respond to Contexts that Shape Practice:						
a. Continuously discover, appraise, and attend to changing locales, populations, scientific and technological developments, and emerging societal trends to provide relevant services						
b. Provide leadership in promoting sustainable changes in service delivery and practice to improve the quality of social services						
EP 2.1.10 Engage, Assess, Intervene, and Evaluate with Individuals, Families, Groups, Organizations and Communities:						
a. Substantively and affectively prepare for action with individuals, families, groups, organizations, and communities						
b. Use empathy and other interpersonal skills						
c. Develop a mutually agreed-on focus of work and desired outcomes						
d. Collect, organize, and interpret client data						
e. Assess client strengths and limitations						
f. Develop mutually agreed-on intervention goals and objectives						
g. Select appropriate intervention strategies						
h. Initiate actions to achieve organizational goals						
i. Implement prevention interventions that enhance client capacities						
j. Help clients resolve problems						
k. Negotiate, mediate, and advocate for clients						
l. Facilitate transitions and endings						
m. Critically analyze, monitor, and evaluate interventions						

Chapter 3: Generalist Social Work Practice

Competencies/Practice Behaviors Exercise 3.1
Violating Confidentiality

Focus Competencies or Practice Behaviors:
- EP 2.1.1c   Attend to professional roles and boundaries
- EP 2.1.2a   Recognize and manage personal values in a way that allows professional values to guide practice
- EP 2.1.2b   Make ethical decisions by applying standards of the National Association of Social Workers Code of Ethics and, as applicable, of the International Federation of Social Workers/International Association of Schools of Social Work Ethics in Social Work, Statement of Principles
- EP 2.1.2d   Apply strategies of ethical reasoning to arrive at principled decisions

A.   Brief Description
   This exercise explores the various aspects of confidentiality in social work.

B.   Objectives
   You will
   1.   Learn guidelines about when to uphold, and when to violate, confidentiality.

C.   Procedure
   1.   Read the following vignette and answer the question raised in this vignette.

> Mary is a social worker in a shelter for battered women. She has just concluded an interview with Ann Jones, a battered mother of three. Mrs. Jones tells Mary that she is going to live with her mother in another state, but that before she goes she is going to get even with her husband for all the hurt he has caused. When Mary asks Mrs. Jones what she intends to do, Mrs. Jones says she is going to burn her husband's house down. When Mary tries to point out the problems this plan will cause Mrs. Jones, the woman says that she doesn't care—her husband deserves it. After saying this, Mrs. Jones bursts out of the office and the shelter, stating she intends to burn the house down this afternoon. Mary is now sitting alone in her office, thinking about this case. What should she do?

   2.   Summarize the course of action you recommend. Indicate legal guidelines, as discussed in the chapter that would require Mary to immediately inform both the police and Mr. Jones (the intended victim) of Mrs. Jones' stated intentions to burn the house down.

Competencies/Practice Behaviors Exercise 3.2
Analyzing a Human Services Organization

Focus Competencies or Practice Behaviors:
- EP 2.1.7a   Utilize conceptual frameworks to guide the processes of assessment, intervention, and evaluation
- EP 2.1.7b   Critique and apply knowledge to understand person and environment
- EP 2.1.9a   Continuously discover, appraise, and attend to changing locales, populations, scientific and technological developments, and emerging societal trends to provide relevant services
- EP 2.1.10a   Substantively and affectively prepare for action with individuals, families, groups, organizations, and communities

A. Brief Description
This exercise is designed to show you how to analyze a human services organization.

B. Objectives
You will:
1. Learn what questions to ask when analyzing an organization.
2. Gain experience interviewing organizational personnel.

C. Procedure
1. You will be required to visit (perhaps in groups of two or three) a human services agency and write a report covering the following information. (Some agencies may not have information or data on one or more questions. If the information is unavailable, you should indicate this in your report.) You will need to call the agency to arrange a meeting. Also, include in your report the name and telephone number of the person with whom you met.
    a. What is the agency's mission statement?
    b. What are its clients' major problems?
    c. What services does the agency provide?
    d. How are client needs determined?
    e. What percentage of clients are people of color, women, gays or lesbians, older adults, or members of other at-risk populations?
    f. What was the total cost of services for the past year?
    g. How much money is spent on each program?
    h. What are the agency's funding sources?
    i. How much and what percentage of funds are received from each source?
    j. What types of clients does the agency refuse?
    k. What other agencies provide the same services in the community?
    l. What is the organizational structure of the agency? For example, is there a formal chain of command?
    m. Is there an informal organization (that is, people who exert a greater amount of influence on decision making than would be expected for their formal position in the bureaucracy)?
    n. How much decision-making input do the direct service providers have on major policy decisions?
    o. Does the agency have a board that oversees its operations? If yes, what are the backgrounds of the board members?
    p. Do employees at every level feel valued?
    q. What is the morale among employees?

r. What are the major unmet needs of the agency?
s. Does the agency have a handbook of personnel policies and procedures?
t. What is the public image of the agency in the community?
u. In recent years what has been the rate of turnover among staff at the agency? What were the major reasons for leaving?
v. Does the agency have a process for evaluating the outcomes of its services? If yes, what is the process, and what are the outcome results?
w. What is the student's overall impression of the agency? For example, if the student needed services that this agency provides, would she or he want to apply at this agency? Why, or why not?

Competencies/Practice Behaviors Exercise 3.3
Role Play—Community Social Work Practice Simulation (Windmere City)

Focus Competencies or Practice Behaviors:
- EP 2.1.2c   Tolerate ambiguity in resolving ethical conflicts
- EP 2.1.2d   Apply strategies of ethical reasoning to arrive at principled decisions
- EP 2.1.3c   Demonstrate effective oral and written communication in working with individuals, families, groups, organizations, communities, and colleagues
- EP 2.1.7a   Utilize conceptual frameworks to guide the processes of assessment, intervention, and evaluation
- EP 2.1.7b   Critique and apply knowledge to understand person and environment

A. Brief Description
This role play is designed to provide an opportunity to experience various aspects of problem-solving in community social work.

B. Objectives
You will:
1. Experience the difficulties involved in satisfying opposing interest groups.
2. Practice community social work techniques in problem solving.

C. Procedure
1. The class will be divided into groups of five and assigned one of the following roles to each group member.
2. Read the following roles and develop the strategy you would use in accomplishing the goals associated with each role.
3. Choose your particular role and portray how you would approach the meeting to best relay your particular interests.

Role List for Windmere City Simulation

Role: Jimmy Hart—Social Worker
　　Your role is to attempt to achieve the goals of your group. Your group is composed of low-income tenants of an apartment building who have come to you because they have no heat in their building. Their landlord is attempting to force them to pay more in rent, claiming that his heating costs have gone up enormously. Tenants realize the landlord's problem but cannot afford to pay a higher rent. You have brought all the parties concerned together for a meeting in the local community center. You will assume responsibility for starting the meeting.

Role: Sly Rich—Apartment Owner
　　Your role is to attempt to get your tenants to pay $20 more per month to help cover your additional heating costs. You have not been successful so far. Your building is 50 years old, poorly insulated, and in need of repairs. You do not like this mess because, as the president of the local Rotary Club, you try to be seen as an upstanding member of the community. The attention being paid to this matter by so many people is becoming embarrassing.

Role: Mary Rule—City Building Inspector
　　Your role is to enforce the building codes of Windmere City. Property owners must maintain their buildings according to certain standards that guarantee the health and safety of their occupants. You don't like to force people to do things but always try to talk them into doing things according to code. Violations of the code carry a fine of $200 per day per violation.

Role: Sal Leeburner—Gas Company Representative
　　Your role is representative of the gas company. Your company is interested in energy efficiency and helping building owners to reduce their energy use. You have a program to loan money at low interest to owners to help them insulate and weatherstrip their buildings.

Role: Oscar Scoop—Investigative Reporter
　　Your role is the consumer investigative reporter for the Windmere television station. You heard that there was a major news story about tenants without any heat and thought it might be a good story for the 6 p.m. news. You also see yourself as helping the "little guys" by focusing attention on their problems.

Chapter 3 Competencies/Practice Behaviors Exercises Assessment:

Name: _____ Date: _____
Supervisor's Name: _____

Focus Competencies/Practice Behaviors:
- EP 2.1.1c   Attend to professional roles and boundaries
- EP 2.1.2a   Recognize and manage personal values in a way that allows professional values to guide practice
- EP 2.1.2b   Make ethical decisions by applying standards of the National Association of Social Workers Code of Ethics and, as applicable, of the International Federation of Social Workers/International Association of Schools of Social Work Ethics in Social Work, Statement of Principles
- EP 2.1.2c   Tolerate ambiguity in resolving ethical conflicts
- EP 2.1.2d   Apply strategies of ethical reasoning to arrive at principled decisions
- EP 2.1.3c   Demonstrate effective oral and written communication in working with individuals, families, groups, organizations, communities, and colleagues
- EP 2.1.7a   Utilize conceptual frameworks to guide the processes of assessment, intervention, and evaluation
- EP 2.1.7b   Critique and apply knowledge to understand person and environment
- EP 2.1.9a   Continuously discover, appraise, and attend to changing locales, populations, scientific and technological developments, and emerging societal trends to provide relevant services
- EP 2.1.10a   Substantively and affectively prepare for action with individuals, families, groups, organizations, and communities

Instructions:
A.   Evaluate your work or your partner's work in the Focus Competencies/Practice Behaviors by completing the Competencies/Practice Behaviors Assessment form below
B.   What other Competencies/Practice Behaviors did you use to complete these Exercises? Be sure to record them in your assessments

1.	I have attained this competency/practice behavior (in the range of 81 to 100%)
2.	I have largely attained this competency/practice behavior (in the range of 61 to 80%)
3.	I have partially attained this competency/practice behavior (in the range of 41 to 60%)
4.	I have made a little progress in attaining this competency/practice behavior (in the range of 21 to 40%)
5.	I have made almost no progress in attaining this competency/practice behavior (in the range of 0 to 20%)

EPAS 2008 Core Competencies & Core Practice Behaviors							Student Self Assessment	Evaluator Feedback
Student and Evaluator Assessment Scale and Comments	0	1	2	3	4	5		Agree/Disagree/Comments
EP 2.1.1 Identify as a Professional Social Worker and Conduct Oneself Accordingly:								
a. Advocate for client access to the services of social work								
b. Practice personal reflection and self-correction to assure continual professional development								
c. Attend to professional roles and boundaries								
d. Demonstrate professional demeanor in behavior, appearance, and communication								
e. Engage in career-long learning								
f. Use supervision and consultation								

EP 2.1.2 Apply Social Work Ethical Principles to Guide Professional Practice:						
a.	Recognize and manage personal values in a way that allows professional values to guide practice					
b.	Make ethical decisions by applying NASW Code of Ethics and, as applicable, of the IFSW/IASSW Ethics in Social Work, Statement of Principles					
c.	Tolerate ambiguity in resolving ethical conflicts					
d.	Apply strategies of ethical reasoning to arrive at principled decisions					
EP 2.1.3 Apply Critical Thinking to Inform and Communicate Professional Judgments:						
a.	Distinguish, appraise, and integrate multiple sources of knowledge, including research-based knowledge and practice wisdom					
b.	Analyze models of assessment, prevention, intervention, and evaluation					
c.	Demonstrate effective oral and written communication in working with individuals, families, groups, organizations, communities, and colleagues					
EP 2.1.4 Engage Diversity and Difference in Practice:						
a.	Recognize the extent to which a culture's structures and values may oppress, marginalize, alienate, or create or enhance privilege and power					
b.	Gain sufficient self-awareness to eliminate the influence of personal biases and values in working with diverse groups					
c.	Recognize and communicate their understanding of the importance of difference in shaping life experiences					
d.	View themselves as learners and engage those with whom they work as informants					
EP 2.1.5 Advance Human Rights and Social and Economic Justice:						
a.	Understand forms and mechanisms of oppression and discrimination					
b.	Advocate for human rights and social and economic justice					
c.	Engage in practices that advance social and economic justice					
EP 2.1.6 Engage in Research-Informed Practice and Practice-Informed Research:						
a.	Use practice experience to inform scientific inquiry					
b.	Use research evidence to inform practice					
EP 2.1.7 Apply Knowledge of Human Behavior and the Social Environment:						
a.	Utilize conceptual frameworks to guide the processes of assessment, intervention, and evaluation					
b.	Critique and apply knowledge to understand person and environment					
EP 2.1.8 Engage in Policy Practice to Advance Social and Economic Well-Being and to Deliver Effective Social Work Services:						
a.	Analyze, formulate, and advocate for policies that advance social well-being					
b.	Collaborate with colleagues and clients for effective policy action					

	EP 2.1.9 Respond to Contexts that Shape Practice:						
a.	Continuously discover, appraise, and attend to changing locales, populations, scientific and technological developments, and emerging societal trends to provide relevant services						
b.	Provide leadership in promoting sustainable changes in service delivery and practice to improve the quality of social services						
	EP 2.1.10 Engage, Assess, Intervene, and Evaluate with Individuals, Families, Groups, Organizations and Communities:						
a.	Substantively and affectively prepare for action with individuals, families, groups, organizations, and communities						
b.	Use empathy and other interpersonal skills						
c.	Develop a mutually agreed-on focus of work and desired outcomes						
d.	Collect, organize, and interpret client data						
e.	Assess client strengths and limitations						
f.	Develop mutually agreed-on intervention goals and objectives						
g.	Select appropriate intervention strategies						
h.	Initiate actions to achieve organizational goals						
i.	Implement prevention interventions that enhance client capacities						
j.	Help clients resolve problems						
k.	Negotiate, mediate, and advocate for clients						
l.	Facilitate transitions and endings						
m.	Critically analyze, monitor, and evaluate interventions						

Chapter 4: Poverty and Public Welfare

Competencies/Practice Behaviors Exercise 4.1
Living on a Public Assistance Budget

Focus Competencies or Practice Behaviors:
- EP 2.1.1b   Practice personal reflection and self-correction to assure continual professional development
- EP 2.1.2a   Recognize and manage personal values in a way that allows professional values to guide practice
- EP 2.1.8a   Analyze, formulate, and advocate for policies that advance social well-being
- EP 2.1.9a   Continuously discover, appraise, and attend to changing locales, populations, scientific and technological developments, and emerging societal trends to provide relevant services

A. Brief Description
    This exercise is designed to have you experience what it is like to live on a welfare budget.

B. Objectives
    You will:
    1. Be more aware of what it is like to be poor.
    2. Practice writing reports.

C. Procedure
    1. Contact a local public assistance office for an estimate of how much money is allocated per week for food and entertainment for an adult who is receiving food stamps and who is a recipient of the state's program that implements the 1996 welfare reform act.
    2. You should restrict your food and entertainment budget to this public assistance level for a week.
    3. After a week, answer the following questions: (a) Did you try to live on this amount? (b) Did you succeed? (c) How did you feel about living on this amount? and (d) What did you learn from this exercise?

Competencies/Practice Behaviors Exercise 4.2
Applying for Public Assistance

Focus Competencies or Practice Behaviors:
- EP 2.1.1b   Practice personal reflection and self-correction to assure continual professional development
- EP 2.1.2a   Recognize and manage personal values in a way that allows professional values to guide practice
- EP 2.1.8a   Analyze, formulate, and advocate for policies that advance social well-being
- EP 2.1.9a   Continuously discover, appraise, and attend to changing locales, populations, scientific and technological developments, and emerging societal trends to provide relevant services

A. Brief Description
This exercise is designed to increase your awareness of what it is like to apply for public assistance.

B. Objectives
You will:
1. Learn what your future clients will experience while working through the welfare system.
2. Practice your writing skills.

C. Procedure
1. Contact a director of the local public assistance agency and ask if you could (with a contrived story) apply for the program in your state that implements the 1996 welfare reform act. The purpose of this simulation is to increase your awareness of the process. If the director gives permission, ask if it would be possible not to inform the agency staff of a possible contrived application so that the experience would be more "real-life" for you.
2. You must have a contrived story (such as "I'm married, have two children, my spouse deserted me, and I'm currently unemployed"). You will need to fill in the details: address, telephone number, age, age of children, and so on. Call the agency to set up an appointment to apply for the program, keep the appointment, go through the interview process, and then inform the agency employee at the end of the interview that the story was contrived in order to learn more about public assistance.
3. Write a report covering the following:
    a. What procedures and processes were involved in applying for assistance?
    b. What kinds of questions were asked by the agency employee?
    c. What were the physical facilities like at the agency?
    d. Were you treated with respect?
    e. Did you feel a stigma attached to applying for assistance?
    f. What was the reaction of the agency employee when informed that the story was contrived?

Competencies/Practice Behaviors Exercise 4.3
Role Play—Cutting Services Due to a Diminished Economy

Focus Competencies or Practice Behaviors:
- EP 2.1.1a   Advocate for client access to the services of social work
- EP 2.1.1b   Practice personal reflection and self-correction to assure continual professional development
- EP 2.1.2c   Tolerate ambiguity in resolving ethical conflicts
- EP 2.1.2d   Apply strategies of ethical reasoning to arrive at principled decisions
- EP 2.1.3c   Demonstrate effective oral and written communication in working with individuals, families, groups, organizations, communities, and colleagues
- EP 2.1.4a   Recognize the extent to which a culture's structures and values may oppress, marginalize, alienate, or create or enhance privilege and power
- EP 2.1.4b   Gain sufficient self-awareness to eliminate the influence of personal biases and values in working with diverse groups
- EP 2.1.5a   Understand forms and mechanisms of oppression and discrimination
- EP 2.1.5b   Advocate for human rights and social and economic justice
- EP 2.1.5c   Engage in practices that advance social and economic justice
- EP 2.1.8a   Analyze, formulate, and advocate for policies that advance social well-being

- EP 2.1.9a   Continuously discover, appraise, and attend to changing locales, populations, scientific and technological developments, and emerging societal trends to provide relevant services
- EP 2.1.9b   Provide leadership in promoting sustainable changes in service delivery and practice to improve the quality of social services
- EP 2.1.10k Negotiate, mediate, and advocate for clients

A. Brief Description
    This role play will demonstrate the difficult decisions involved in making budget cuts.

B. Objectives
    You will:
    1. Experience group decision making.
    2. Practice oral communication skills.

C. Procedure
    1. Select eleven classmates—one mediator and one person representing each of the following programs in the vignette below.
    2. Each person should research their program and be ready to explain why your program should not be cut.
    3. Following this role play, discuss the difficulties in advocating for your program while knowing other programs would be cut if yours was not.

> **Mediator role:** A worker who provides intervention in disputes between parties to help them find compromises, reconciles differences, or reach mutually satisfactory agreements
>
> **Food Stamps:** A public assistance program that is designed to combat hunger and to improve the diets of low-income households by supplementing their food-purchasing ability
>
> **General Assistance:** This public assistance program is supposed to serve those needing temporary, rather than long-term, financial support. This is the only public assistance program that receives no federal funds, instead is usually funded by property taxes
>
> **Housing Assistance:** Similar to food stamps and Medicaid, this public assistance program is an in-kind program rather than a cash program by providing public housing or help with renting and even buying homes
>
> **Medicaid:** This public assistance program provides hospital and medical care to certain poverty-stricken people, and is a joint federal/state program
>
> **Medicare:** This is Title XVIII to the Social Security Act, it has two parts: hospital insurance that is financed by a surcharge on the Social Security Taxes paid by employers and employees; and the medical insurance part, which is a voluntary plan for which enrollees are charged a monthly premium
>
> **Old Age, Survivors, Disability, and Health Insurance (OASDHI):** A social insurance program created by the Social Security Act and usually referred to as Social Security by the public. It is designed to partially replace income that is lost when a worker retires or becomes disabled

Supplemental Security Income (SSI): In this public assistance program the federal government pays monthly checks to people in financial need who are 65 years of age and older or who are blind or disabled at any age

Temporary Assistance to Needy Families (TANF): This public assistance program replaced AFDC, with the assumption that in order to avoid a long-term welfare class, all jobless people should work

Unemployment Insurance: A program of the Social Security Act, it provides benefits to workers who have been laid off or, in certain cases, fired. It is financed by a tax on employers

Workers' Compensation Insurance: This program provides both income and assistance in meeting medical expenses for injuries sustained on a job. By 1948 all states had adequate coverage

Chapter 4 Competencies/Practice Behaviors Exercises Assessment:

Name: _____ Date: _____
Supervisor's Name: _____

Focus Competencies/Practice Behaviors:
- EP 2.1.1a   Advocate for client access to the services of social work
- EP 2.1.1b   Practice personal reflection and self-correction to assure continual professional development
- EP 2.1.2a   Recognize and manage personal values in a way that allows professional values to guide practice
- EP 2.1.2c   Tolerate ambiguity in resolving ethical conflicts
- EP 2.1.2d   Apply strategies of ethical reasoning to arrive at principled decisions
- EP 2.1.3c   Demonstrate effective oral and written communication in working with individuals, families, groups, organizations, communities, and colleagues
- EP 2.1.4a   Recognize the extent to which a culture's structures and values may oppress, marginalize, alienate, or create or enhance privilege and power
- EP 2.1.4b   Gain sufficient self-awareness to eliminate the influence of personal biases and values in working with diverse groups
- EP 2.1.5a   Understand forms and mechanisms of oppression and discrimination
- EP 2.1.5b   Advocate for human rights and social and economic justice
- EP 2.1.5c   Engage in practices that advance social and economic justice
- EP 2.1.8a   Analyze, formulate, and advocate for policies that advance social well-being
- EP 2.1.9a   Continuously discover, appraise, and attend to changing locales, populations, scientific and technological developments, and emerging societal trends to provide relevant services
- EP 2.1.9b   Provide leadership in promoting sustainable changes in service delivery and practice to improve the quality of social services
- EP 2.1.10k   Negotiate, mediate, and advocate for clients

Instructions:
A.   Evaluate your work or your partner's work in the Focus Competencies/Practice Behaviors by completing the Competencies/Practice Behaviors Assessment form below
B.   What other Competencies/Practice Behaviors did you use to complete these Exercises? Be sure to record them in your assessments

1.	I have attained this competency/practice behavior (in the range of 81 to 100%)
2.	I have largely attained this competency/practice behavior (in the range of 61 to 80%)
3.	I have partially attained this competency/practice behavior (in the range of 41 to 60%)
4.	I have made a little progress in attaining this competency/practice behavior (in the range of 21 to 40%)
5.	I have made almost no progress in attaining this competency/practice behavior (in the range of 0 to 20%)

EPAS 2008 Core Competencies & Core Practice Behaviors	Student Self Assessment						Evaluator Feedback
Student and Evaluator Assessment Scale and Comments	0	1	2	3	4	5	Agree/Disagree/Comments
EP 2.1.1 Identify as a Professional Social Worker and Conduct Oneself Accordingly:							
a. Advocate for client access to the services of social work							
b. Practice personal reflection and self-correction to assure continual professional development							

c.	Attend to professional roles and boundaries							
d.	Demonstrate professional demeanor in behavior, appearance, and communication							
e.	Engage in career-long learning							
f.	Use supervision and consultation							
EP 2.1.2 Apply Social Work Ethical Principles to Guide Professional Practice:								
a.	Recognize and manage personal values in a way that allows professional values to guide practice							
b.	Make ethical decisions by applying NASW Code of Ethics and, as applicable, of the IFSW/IASSW Ethics in Social Work, Statement of Principles							
c.	Tolerate ambiguity in resolving ethical conflicts							
d.	Apply strategies of ethical reasoning to arrive at principled decisions							
EP 2.1.3 Apply Critical Thinking to Inform and Communicate Professional Judgments:								
a.	Distinguish, appraise, and integrate multiple sources of knowledge, including research-based knowledge and practice wisdom							
b.	Analyze models of assessment, prevention, intervention, and evaluation							
c.	Demonstrate effective oral and written communication in working with individuals, families, groups, organizations, communities, and colleagues							
EP 2.1.4 Engage Diversity and Difference in Practice:								
a.	Recognize the extent to which a culture's structures and values may oppress, marginalize, alienate, or create or enhance privilege and power							
b.	Gain sufficient self-awareness to eliminate the influence of personal biases and values in working with diverse groups							
c.	Recognize and communicate their understanding of the importance of difference in shaping life experiences							
d.	View themselves as learners and engage those with whom they work as informants							
EP 2.1.5 Advance Human Rights and Social and Economic Justice:								
a.	Understand forms and mechanisms of oppression and discrimination							
b.	Advocate for human rights and social and economic justice							
c.	Engage in practices that advance social and economic justice							
EP 2.1.6 Engage in Research-Informed Practice and Practice-Informed Research:								
a.	Use practice experience to inform scientific inquiry							
b.	Use research evidence to inform practice							
EP 2.1.7 Apply Knowledge of Human Behavior and the Social Environment:								
a.	Utilize conceptual frameworks to guide the processes of assessment, intervention, and evaluation							
b.	Critique and apply knowledge to understand person and environment							

EP 2.1.8 Engage in Policy Practice to Advance Social and Economic Well-Being and to Deliver Effective Social Work Services:					
a. Analyze, formulate, and advocate for policies that advance social well-being					
b. Collaborate with colleagues and clients for effective policy action					
EP 2.1.9 Respond to Contexts that Shape Practice:					
a. Continuously discover, appraise, and attend to changing locales, populations, scientific and technological developments, and emerging societal trends to provide relevant services					
b. Provide leadership in promoting sustainable changes in service delivery and practice to improve the quality of social services					
EP 2.1.10 Engage, Assess, Intervene, and Evaluate with Individuals, Families, Groups, Organizations and Communities:					
a. Substantively and affectively prepare for action with individuals, families, groups, organizations, and communities					
b. Use empathy and other interpersonal skills					
c. Develop a mutually agreed-on focus of work and desired outcomes					
d. Collect, organize, and interpret client data					
e. Assess client strengths and limitations					
f. Develop mutually agreed-on intervention goals and objectives					
g. Select appropriate intervention strategies					
h. Initiate actions to achieve organizational goals					
i. Implement prevention interventions that enhance client capacities					
j. Help clients resolve problems					
k. Negotiate, mediate, and advocate for clients					
l. Facilitate transitions and endings					
m. Critically analyze, monitor, and evaluate interventions					

Chapter 5: Emotional/Behavioral Problems and Counseling

Competencies/Practice Behaviors Exercise 5.1
Understanding Bizarre Behavior

Focus Competencies or Practice Behaviors:
- EP 2.1.3a Distinguish, appraise, and integrate multiple sources of knowledge, including research-based knowledge and practice wisdom
- EP 2.1.3c Demonstrate effective oral and written communication in working with individuals, families, groups, organizations, communities, and colleagues
- EP 2.1.7a Utilize conceptual frameworks to guide the processes of assessment, intervention, and evaluation
- EP 2.1.7b Critique and apply knowledge to understand person and environment
- EP 2.1.10a Substantively and affectively prepare for action with individuals, families, groups, organizations, and communities

A. Brief Description
    This exercise is designed to help you learn how to conceptualize why unusual behaviors occur.

B. Objectives
    You will:
    1. Research articles regarding bizarre behaviors.
    2. Practice report writing.

C. Procedure
    1. Search for information from the Internet, books, magazines, or newspaper articles as to the reasons why someone committed a bizarre act that received national attention. (Examples include John Hinckley's shooting of former President Reagan in 1981, Lorena Bobbitt's slicing off her husband's penis in 1993, and the Denver massacre at the Batman movie in 2012.)
    2. Write a brief report (no longer than a page in length) summarizing the reasons, and your thoughts about those reasons.

Competencies/Practice Behaviors Exercise 5.2
Debate over the Existence of Mental Illness

Focus Competencies or Practice Behaviors:
- EP 2.1.3a Distinguish, appraise, and integrate multiple sources of knowledge, including research-based knowledge and practice wisdom
- EP 2.1.7a Utilize conceptual frameworks to guide the processes of assessment, intervention, and evaluation
- EP 2.1.7b Critique and apply knowledge to understand person and environment
- EP 2.1.10a Substantively and affectively prepare for action with individuals, families, groups, organizations, and communities

A. Brief Description
This exercise is designed to help you examine both sides of the question as to whether mental illness exists.

B. Objectives
You will:
1. Research articles regarding the issue of mental illness.
2. Practice report writing.

C. Procedure
1. Read the material in the text regarding the issue of mental illness, and whether it really exists.
2. Research this issue in articles and books. Write a paper summarizing your beliefs on this issue.

Competencies/Practice Behaviors Exercise 5.3
Changing Unwanted Emotions by Writing a Rational Self-Analysis

Focus Competencies or Practice Behaviors:
- EP 2.1.3a Distinguish, appraise, and integrate multiple sources of knowledge, including research-based knowledge and practice wisdom
- EP 2.1.6a Use practice experience to inform scientific inquiry
- EP 2.1.7a Utilize conceptual frameworks to guide the processes of assessment, intervention, and evaluation
- EP 2.1.7b Critique and apply knowledge to understand person and environment
- EP 2.1.10a Substantively and affectively prepare for action with individuals, families, groups, organizations, and communities
- EP 2.1.10d Collect, organize, and interpret client data
- EP 2.1.10e Assess client strengths and limitations
- EP 2.1.10g Select appropriate intervention strategies
- EP 2.1.10j Help clients resolve problems
- EP 2.1.10m Critically analyze, monitor, and evaluate interventions

A. Brief Description
This exercise is designed to help you understand that unwanted emotions primarily result from negative and irrational thinking, and that unwanted emotions can be changed by challenging negative and irrational thinking with positive and rational self-talk.

B. Objectives
You will:
1. Understand negative and irrational thinking.
2. Learn how to write a rational self-analysis.

C. Procedure
1. Read the material in the text on how to write a rational self-analysis.
2. Write a rational self-analysis on an unwanted emotion that you are currently experiencing, or have recently experienced.

Competencies/Practice Behaviors Exercise 5.4
Role Play—Learning to Counsel

Focus Competencies or Practice Behaviors:
- EP 2.1.7a Utilize conceptual frameworks to guide the processes of assessment, intervention, and evaluation
- EP 2.1.10a Substantively and affectively prepare for action with individuals, families, groups, organizations, and communities
- EP 2.1.10b Use empathy and other interpersonal skills
- EP 2.1.10c Develop a mutually agreed-on focus of work and desired outcomes
- EP 2.1.10d Collect, organize, and interpret client data
- EP 2.1.10e Assess client strengths and limitations
- EP 2.1.10f Develop mutually agreed-on intervention goals and objectives
- EP 2.1.10g Select appropriate intervention strategies
- EP 2.1.10i Implement prevention interventions that enhance client capacities
- EP 2.1.10j Help clients resolve problems
- EP 2.1.10l Facilitate transitions and endings

A. Brief Description

The purpose of this exercise is to help you learn how to interview and counsel through role playing.

B. Objectives

You will:
1. Learn the phases of the counseling process.
2. Observe the instructor role play a counseling situation.
3. Participate in role-playing a counseling session.

C. Procedure
1. The instructor will briefly describe the counseling process as comprising the following phases:
    a. Building a relationship
    b. Exploring the problems in depth
    c. Exploring alternatives
2. The instructor will demonstrate these three phases through counseling two students with a contrived problem. (The instructor should not be informed what problem has been chosen.)
3. Students will then be asked to jointly role play contrived problems at the next class period. Examples of such problems include the following:
    a. A student is concerned that his or her roommate has a drinking problem that the other denies.
    b. A couple is married. The wife wants to become a surrogate mother, but her husband objects.
    c. A brother and sister are worried about their elderly mother who is living alone in her home. Her health is failing, and she is increasingly forgetful. The brother wants to seek a nursing home placement for his mother, but the sister objects.
4. The class will then discuss the merits and shortcomings of the counseling that was provided.

Chapter 5 Competencies/Practice Behaviors Exercises Assessment:

Name: _____ Date: _____

Supervisor's Name: _____

Focus Competencies/Practice Behaviors:
- EP 2.1.3a   Distinguish, appraise, and integrate multiple sources of knowledge, including research-based knowledge and practice wisdom
- EP 2.1.3c   Demonstrate effective oral and written communication in working with individuals, families, groups, organizations, communities, and colleagues
- EP 2.1.6a   Use practice experience to inform scientific inquiry
- EP 2.1.7a   Utilize conceptual frameworks to guide the processes of assessment, intervention, and evaluation
- EP 2.1.7b   Critique and apply knowledge to understand person and environment
- EP 2.1.10a Substantively and affectively prepare for action with individuals, families, groups, organizations, and communities
- EP 2.1.10b Use empathy and other interpersonal skills
- EP 2.1.10c Develop a mutually agreed-on focus of work and desired outcomes
- EP 2.1.10d Collect, organize, and interpret client data
- EP 2.1.10e Assess client strengths and limitations
- EP 2.1.10f Develop mutually agreed-on intervention goals and objectives
- EP 2.1.10g Select appropriate intervention strategies
- EP 2.1.10i Implement prevention interventions that enhance client capacities
- EP 2.1.10j Help clients resolve problems
- EP 2.1.10l Facilitate transitions and endings
- EP 2.1.10m Critically analyze, monitor, and evaluate interventions

Instructions:
A. Evaluate your work or your partner's work in the Focus Competencies/Practice Behaviors by completing the Competencies/Practice Behaviors Assessment form below
B. What other Competencies/Practice Behaviors did you use to complete these Exercises? Be sure to record them in your assessments

1.	I have attained this competency/practice behavior (in the range of 81 to 100%)
2.	I have largely attained this competency/practice behavior (in the range of 61 to 80%)
3.	I have partially attained this competency/practice behavior (in the range of 41 to 60%)
4.	I have made a little progress in attaining this competency/practice behavior (in the range of 21 to 40%)
5.	I have made almost no progress in attaining this competency/practice behavior (in the range of 0 to 20%)

EPAS 2008 Core Competencies & Core Practice Behaviors	Student Self Assessment						Evaluator Feedback
Student and Evaluator Assessment Scale and Comments	0	1	2	3	4	5	Agree/Disagree/Comments
EP 2.1.1 Identify as a Professional Social Worker and Conduct Oneself Accordingly:							
a. Advocate for client access to the services of social work							
b. Practice personal reflection and self-correction to assure continual professional development							
c. Attend to professional roles and boundaries							

d.	Demonstrate professional demeanor in behavior, appearance, and communication						
e.	Engage in career-long learning						
f.	Use supervision and consultation						
EP 2.1.2 Apply Social Work Ethical Principles to Guide Professional Practice:							
a.	Recognize and manage personal values in a way that allows professional values to guide practice						
b.	Make ethical decisions by applying NASW Code of Ethics and, as applicable, of the IFSW/IASSW Ethics in Social Work, Statement of Principles						
c.	Tolerate ambiguity in resolving ethical conflicts						
d.	Apply strategies of ethical reasoning to arrive at principled decisions						
EP 2.1.3 Apply Critical Thinking to Inform and Communicate Professional Judgments:							
a.	Distinguish, appraise, and integrate multiple sources of knowledge, including research-based knowledge and practice wisdom						
b.	Analyze models of assessment, prevention, intervention, and evaluation						
c.	Demonstrate effective oral and written communication in working with individuals, families, groups, organizations, communities, and colleagues						
EP 2.1.4 Engage Diversity and Difference in Practice:							
a.	Recognize the extent to which a culture's structures and values may oppress, marginalize, alienate, or create or enhance privilege and power						
b.	Gain sufficient self-awareness to eliminate the influence of personal biases and values in working with diverse groups						
c.	Recognize and communicate their understanding of the importance of difference in shaping life experiences						
d.	View themselves as learners and engage those with whom they work as informants						
EP 2.1.5 Advance Human Rights and Social and Economic Justice:							
a.	Understand forms and mechanisms of oppression and discrimination						
b.	Advocate for human rights and social and economic justice						
c.	Engage in practices that advance social and economic justice						
EP 2.1.6 Engage in Research-Informed Practice and Practice-Informed Research:							
a.	Use practice experience to inform scientific inquiry						
b.	Use research evidence to inform practice						
EP 2.1.7 Apply Knowledge of Human Behavior and the Social Environment:							
a.	Utilize conceptual frameworks to guide the processes of assessment, intervention, and evaluation						
b.	Critique and apply knowledge to understand person and environment						

EP 2.1.8 Engage in Policy Practice to Advance Social and Economic Well-Being and to Deliver Effective Social Work Services:					
a. Analyze, formulate, and advocate for policies that advance social well-being					
b. Collaborate with colleagues and clients for effective policy action					
EP 2.1.9 Respond to Contexts that Shape Practice:					
a. Continuously discover, appraise, and attend to changing locales, populations, scientific and technological developments, and emerging societal trends to provide relevant services					
b. Provide leadership in promoting sustainable changes in service delivery and practice to improve the quality of social services					
EP 2.1.10 Engage, Assess, Intervene, and Evaluate with Individuals, Families, Groups, Organizations and Communities:					
a. Substantively and affectively prepare for action with individuals, families, groups, organizations, and communities					
b. Use empathy and other interpersonal skills					
c. Develop a mutually agreed-on focus of work and desired outcomes					
d. Collect, organize, and interpret client data					
e. Assess client strengths and limitations					
f. Develop mutually agreed-on intervention goals and objectives					
g. Select appropriate intervention strategies					
h. Initiate actions to achieve organizational goals					
i. Implement prevention interventions that enhance client capacities					
j. Help clients resolve problems					
k. Negotiate, mediate, and advocate for clients					
l. Facilitate transitions and endings					
m. Critically analyze, monitor, and evaluate interventions					

Chapter 6: Family Problems and Services to Families

Competencies/Practice Behaviors Exercise 6.1
Is It Romantic Love or Rational Love?

Focus Competencies or Practice Behaviors:
- EP 2.1.1b   Practice personal reflection and self-correction to assure continual professional development
- EP 2.1.2a   Recognize and manage personal values in a way that allows professional values to guide practice
- EP 2.1.3a   Distinguish, appraise, and integrate multiple sources of knowledge, including research-based knowledge and practice wisdom
- EP 2.1.7a   Utilize conceptual frameworks to guide the processes of assessment, intervention, and evaluation

A. Brief Description
   This exercise is designed to have you analyze the nature of a relationship with someone with whom you are (or were) "in love."

B. Objectives
   You will:
   1. Learn the difference between romantic love and rational love.

C. Procedure
   1. Write on a sheet of paper the following information about someone with whom you are "in love." If some of you are not currently "in love," write down the following information about someone you were "in love" with in the past. (You will not be asked to share this information with anyone other the instructor, unless you provide permission to do so.)

The Reasons I Am (or Was) Attracted to This Person Are:	*The Things I Find Irritating About This Person Are:*
1.	1.
2.	2.
3.	3.
4.	4.
5.	5.
6. ...	6. ...

   2. Examine what you wrote and write a statement regarding whether your relationship is primarily one of romantic love or rational love.

Competencies/Practice Behaviors Exercise 6.2
Family Problems and Tragedy

Focus Competencies or Practice Behaviors:
- EP 2.1.1b   Practice personal reflection and self-correction to assure continual professional development
- EP 2.1.2a   Recognize and manage personal values in a way that allows professional values to guide practice
- EP 2.1.2b   Make ethical decisions by applying standards of the National Association of Social Workers Code of Ethics and, as applicable, of the International Federation of Social Workers/International Association of Schools of Social Work Ethics in Social Work, Statement of Principles
- EP 2.1.2d   Apply strategies of ethical reasoning to arrive at principled decisions
- EP 2.1.4a   Recognize the extent to which a culture's structures and values may oppress, marginalize, alienate, or create or enhance privilege and power
- EP 2.1.4b   Gain sufficient self-awareness to eliminate the influence of personal biases and values in working with diverse groups
- EP 2.1.5a   Understand forms and mechanisms of oppression and discrimination
- EP 2.1.7a   Utilize conceptual frameworks to guide the processes of assessment, intervention, and evaluation
- EP 2.1.7b   Critique and apply knowledge to understand person and environment

A. Brief Description
   This exercise is designed to have you examine your values about several family issues.

B. Objectives
   You will:
   1. Experience the difficulties involved in "placing blame/responsibility" with regard to family issues.
   2. Examine your personal values.

C. Procedure
   1. Rank the following people with respect to responsibility for Rachel's death. The ranking is from 6 (least responsible) to 1 (most responsible). Read the following vignette twice.

   > Rachel is 19 years old and is an attractive, white, college sophomore. She believes strongly in racial equality and begins dating Kim (a sophomore student from Korea). Because her parents have told her on several occasions that they are strongly opposed to interracial dating and marriage, she intentionally does not inform her parents that she is dating Kim.
   >
   > Rachel becomes pregnant. Kim informs her that he wants to marry her. He adds that after they graduate, it will be necessary for them to spend at least a few years in Korea. Kim also adds that his parents may initially object to the marriage, because they have mentioned on a few occasions that it would not be proper for him to marry someone who is not Korean. Neither Kim nor Rachel has the money to pay for an abortion.
   >
   > Rachel decides she is not yet ready to get married, and she is uncertain whether she wants to live in a foreign country. She therefore goes home with the intention of informing her parents that she is pregnant and needs $300 to obtain an abortion. She begins by telling her mother that she is dating Kim and that she has on a few occasions stayed overnight at his apartment. Her mother becomes visibly upset and calls in her

> husband. Both parents angrily inform Rachel that she must immediately stop dating Kim or they will financially force her to drop out of attending college. Her parents' reaction is so emotional that she decides not to inform them of her pregnancy. Rachel also fears that if she tells her parents, her father may physically hit her, as he has done in the past when he is intensely upset.
>
> Rachel returns to college very confused and distraught. Two days later she hears of someone who will perform the abortion for one-third the normal price. Kim and Rachel borrow the necessary money from their friends. They go together to the abortionist. Unknown to Kim and Rachel, the abortionist has had no formal medical training and is fairly unskilled. Rachel begins hemorrhaging shortly after the abortion. Kim rushes her to the nearest hospital, but it is too late to save her life. The hospital administrator urges Kim to inform the police about the abortionist; she adds that Rachel was the fourth person who has been admitted to the hospital after being treated by this abortionist—the other three lived. Neither Kim nor the hospital administrator follows through in informing the police.

2. Rank who you believe is most to least responsible for Rachel's death (a ranking of 1 is the most responsible).

   ____ Rachel
   ____ Kim
   ____ Rachel's father
   ____ Rachel's mother
   ____ The abortionist
   ____ The hospital administrator

3. Explain the reasons for your ranking.

Competencies/Practice Behaviors Exercise 6.3
Family Values

Focus Competencies or Practice Behaviors:

- EP 2.1.1b   Practice personal reflection and self-correction to assure continual professional development
- EP 2.1.3a   Distinguish, appraise, and integrate multiple sources of knowledge, including research-based knowledge and practice wisdom
- EP 2.1.4a   Recognize the extent to which a culture's structures and values may oppress, marginalize, alienate, or create or enhance privilege and power
- EP 2.1.4b   Gain sufficient self-awareness to eliminate the influence of personal biases and values in working with diverse groups
- EP 2.1.4c   Recognize and communicate their understanding of the importance of difference in shaping life experiences
- EP 2.1.4d   View themselves as learners and engage those with whom they work as informants
- EP 2.1.5a   Understand forms and mechanisms of oppression and discrimination
- EP 2.1.7a   Utilize conceptual frameworks to guide the processes of assessment, intervention, and evaluation
- EP 2.1.8a   Analyze, formulate, and advocate for policies that advance social well-being
- EP 2.1.10a   Substantively and affectively prepare for action with individuals, families, groups, organizations, and communities

A. Brief Description
This exercise is designed to help you clarify your values related to marriage and family.

B. Objectives
You will:
1. Clarify your personal values regarding marriage and family.
2. Practice your writing skills.

C. Procedure
1. Using the following scale, circle the number that best exemplifies your beliefs.

   1   Definitely not
   2   Probably not
   3   Probably yes
   4   Definitely yes

   1. Would you marry someone of a different race?
      1   2   3   4

   2. Would you marry someone whose religion differs from yours?
      1   2   3   4

   3. If you were going to adopt a child, would you adopt a child of a different race?
      1   2   3   4

   4. If you were in an empty-shell marriage, would you seriously consider getting a divorce?
      1   2   3   4

   5. If your spouse had an extramarital affair (and asked for your forgiveness), would you seek a divorce?
      1   2   3   4

   6. Do you believe the husband should be the primary wage-earner in a family?
      1   2   3   4

   7. Do you believe the wife should have the primary responsibility for taking care of the young children in a family?
      1   2   3   4

   8. Do you believe wives should have the primary responsibility for doing most of the household domestic tasks?
      1   2   3   4

   9. Do you believe there are some circumstances (other than to save the life of the mother) for which abortion is justifiable?
      1   2   3   4

10. Do you believe that every father who commits incest with a daughter should be placed in jail?
       1   2   3   4

11. Do you support a constitutional amendment to make abortions illegal?
       1   2   3   4

12. Would you be willing sometime in the future to be a surrogate mother? If you are a male, would you be willing to have your wife or future wife become a surrogate mother?
       1   2   3   4

13. Do you believe our government should support an extensive program to develop the capacity to clone human beings?
       1   2   3   4

14. Do you believe people should retain their virginity until they marry?
       1   2   3   4

15. Do you believe there are some circumstances (such as a spouse being physically incapacitated) that justify a married person having an extramarital affair?
       1   2   3   4

16. Would you object to your son having premarital sex?
       1   2   3   4

17. Would you object to your daughter having premarital sex?
       1   2   3   4

18. Do you think the government should help support day-care centers for working mothers?
       1   2   3   4

19. Do you approve of a young couple trying out marriage by living together before actually getting married?
       1   2   3   4

20. Do you think people should limit the size of their families to two children?
       1   2   3   4

21. Do you favor a law to limit families to two children?
       1   2   3   4

22. Would you consider marrying someone who is divorced and has two young children (assume you are single)?
       1   2   3   4

23. Do you believe unmarried teenage mothers should, in most circumstances, place their children for adoption?
       1   2   3   4

> 24. Do you believe gay and lesbian couples should be allowed to marry?
>   1   2   3   4
>
> 25. Do you believe gays and lesbians should generally be allowed to raise their children?
>   1   2   3   4
>
> 26. Do you believe it is desirable for Planned Parenthood clinics to be physically located in high schools in order to attempt to reduce the number of teenage pregnancies?
>   1   2   3   4
>
> 27. Do you believe married couples should be expected to have children?
>   1   2   3   4
>
> 28. Do you support co-marital sex (that is, mate swapping)?
>   1   2   3   4

2. After you have answered the questions, write a report explaining your rankings for each question.

Competencies/Practice Behaviors Exercise 6.4
Role Play—The Problem with Lynn

Focus Competencies or Practice Behaviors:
- EP 2.1.1b Practice personal reflection and self-correction to assure continual professional development
- EP 2.1.1d Demonstrate professional demeanor in behavior, appearance, and communication
- EP 2.1.2a Recognize and manage personal values in a way that allows professional values to guide practice
- EP 2.1.2b Make ethical decisions by applying standards of the National Association of Social Workers Code of Ethics and, as applicable, of the International Federation of Social Workers/International Association of Schools of Social Work Ethics in Social Work, Statement of Principles
- EP 2.1.3a Distinguish, appraise, and integrate multiple sources of knowledge, including research-based knowledge and practice wisdom
- EP 2.1.10a Substantively and affectively prepare for action with individuals, families, groups, organizations, and communities
- EP 2.1.10b Use empathy and other interpersonal skills

A. Brief Description
   This role play is designed to have you share and examine your views on such issues as premarital pregnancy, abortion, family violence, early marriage, and related matters.

B. Objectives
   You will:
   1. Contemplate the issue of abortion.
   2. Practice your oral communication and persuasion.

C. Procedure
1. Form groups of five.
2. Read the following "Problem with Lynn Situation Sheet."

> The Problem with Lynn Situation Sheet
>
> Lynn is a 16-year-old who is six weeks pregnant. The father of the fetus is Todd, an 18-year-old who works as a part-time janitor at a local company. He is a high school dropout but has gotten his GED at the technical school. Lynn is a junior in high school. Lynn has not told her parents about the pregnancy. Her father has a reputation for abusing his wife, and Lynn is afraid to talk to him. Her mother is a passive person; Lynn does not feel she would be helpful in this situation. Todd wants to get married and raise the child. Lynn is not sure she is ready to be married or to have a child. Lynn and Todd argue about what to do. Kim, Lynn's friend, suggests an abortion. Todd objects. Lynn decides that an abortion is the best solution and arranges to have this done. (Lynn lives in a state in which she does not have to have parental consent in order to have an abortion.) When she tells Todd that she has had an abortion, he explodes, punches her, and takes off. The next day he asks Lynn to forgive him and brings her flowers and a beautiful sweater.

3. Based on the facts presented above, begin the role plays by each group member explaining to the group his or her responses to the following questions:
   a. What would you predict about the future of Lynn's and Todd's relationship if she gets back together with him?
   b. Was Lynn right or wrong in having the abortion against Todd's wishes?
   c. Was Todd justified in hitting Lynn because of what she did?
   d. Was Lynn right in not telling her parents about the abortion?

Chapter 6 Competencies/Practice Behaviors Exercises Assessment:

Name: _____ **Date:** _____
Supervisor's Name: _____

Focus Competencies/Practice Behaviors:
- EP 2.1.1b Practice personal reflection and self-correction to assure continual professional development
- EP 2.1.1d Demonstrate professional demeanor in behavior, appearance, and communication
- EP 2.1.2a Recognize and manage personal values in a way that allows professional values to guide practice
- EP 2.1.2b Make ethical decisions by applying standards of the National Association of Social Workers Code of Ethics and, as applicable, of the International Federation of Social Workers/International Association of Schools of Social Work Ethics in Social Work, Statement of Principles
- EP 2.1.2d Apply strategies of ethical reasoning to arrive at principled decisions
- EP 2.1.3a Distinguish, appraise, and integrate multiple sources of knowledge, including research-based knowledge and practice wisdom
- EP 2.1.4a Recognize the extent to which a culture's structures and values may oppress, marginalize, alienate, or create or enhance privilege and power
- EP 2.1.4b Gain sufficient self-awareness to eliminate the influence of personal biases and values in working with diverse groups
- EP 2.1.4c Recognize and communicate their understanding of the importance of difference in shaping life experiences
- EP 2.1.4d View themselves as learners and engage those with whom they work as informants
- EP 2.1.5a Understand forms and mechanisms of oppression and discrimination
- EP 2.1.7a Utilize conceptual frameworks to guide the processes of assessment, intervention, and evaluation
- EP 2.1.7b Critique and apply knowledge to understand person and environment
- EP 2.1.8a Analyze, formulate, and advocate for policies that advance social well-being
- EP 2.1.10a Substantively and affectively prepare for action with individuals, families, groups, organizations, and communities
- EP 2.1.10b Use empathy and other interpersonal skills

Instructions:
A. Evaluate your work or your partner's work in the Focus Competencies/Practice Behaviors by completing the Competencies/Practice Behaviors Assessment form below
B. What other Competencies/Practice Behaviors did you use to complete these Exercises? Be sure to record them in your assessments

1.	I have attained this competency/practice behavior (in the range of 81 to 100%)
2.	I have largely attained this competency/practice behavior (in the range of 61 to 80%)
3.	I have partially attained this competency/practice behavior (in the range of 41 to 60%)
4.	I have made a little progress in attaining this competency/practice behavior (in the range of 21 to 40%)
5.	I have made almost no progress in attaining this competency/practice behavior (in the range of 0 to 20%)

EPAS 2008 Core Competencies & Core Practice Behaviors	Student Self Assessment						Evaluator Feedback
Student and Evaluator Assessment Scale and Comments	0	1	2	3	4	5	Agree/Disagree/Comments
EP 2.1.1 Identify as a Professional Social Worker and Conduct Oneself Accordingly:							
a. Advocate for client access to the services of social work							
b. Practice personal reflection and self-correction to assure continual professional development							
c. Attend to professional roles and boundaries							
d. Demonstrate professional demeanor in behavior, appearance, and communication							
e. Engage in career-long learning							
f. Use supervision and consultation							
EP 2.1.2 Apply Social Work Ethical Principles to Guide Professional Practice:							
a. Recognize and manage personal values in a way that allows professional values to guide practice							
b. Make ethical decisions by applying NASW Code of Ethics and, as applicable, of the IFSW/IASSW Ethics in Social Work, Statement of Principles							
c. Tolerate ambiguity in resolving ethical conflicts							
d. Apply strategies of ethical reasoning to arrive at principled decisions							
EP 2.1.3 Apply Critical Thinking to Inform and Communicate Professional Judgments:							
a. Distinguish, appraise, and integrate multiple sources of knowledge, including research-based knowledge and practice wisdom							
b. Analyze models of assessment, prevention, intervention, and evaluation							
c. Demonstrate effective oral and written communication in working with individuals, families, groups, organizations, communities, and colleagues							
EP 2.1.4 Engage Diversity and Difference in Practice:							
a. Recognize the extent to which a culture's structures and values may oppress, marginalize, alienate, or create or enhance privilege and power							
b. Gain sufficient self-awareness to eliminate the influence of personal biases and values in working with diverse groups							
c. Recognize and communicate their understanding of the importance of difference in shaping life experiences							
d. View themselves as learners and engage those with whom they work as informants							
EP 2.1.5 Advance Human Rights and Social and Economic Justice:							
a. Understand forms and mechanisms of oppression and discrimination							
b. Advocate for human rights and social and economic justice							
c. Engage in practices that advance social and economic justice							
EP 2.1.6 Engage in Research-Informed Practice and Practice-Informed Research:							
a. Use practice experience to inform scientific inquiry							
b. Use research evidence to inform practice							

EP 2.1.7 Apply Knowledge of Human Behavior and the Social Environment:						
a.	Utilize conceptual frameworks to guide the processes of assessment, intervention, and evaluation					
b.	Critique and apply knowledge to understand person and environment					
EP 2.1.8 Engage in Policy Practice to Advance Social and Economic Well-Being and to Deliver Effective Social Work Services:						
a.	Analyze, formulate, and advocate for policies that advance social well-being					
b.	Collaborate with colleagues and clients for effective policy action					
EP 2.1.9 Respond to Contexts that Shape Practice:						
a.	Continuously discover, appraise, and attend to changing locales, populations, scientific and technological developments, and emerging societal trends to provide relevant services					
b.	Provide leadership in promoting sustainable changes in service delivery and practice to improve the quality of social services					
EP 2.1.10 Engage, Assess, Intervene, and Evaluate with Individuals, Families, Groups, Organizations and Communities:						
a.	Substantively and affectively prepare for action with individuals, families, groups, organizations, and communities					
b.	Use empathy and other interpersonal skills					
c.	Develop a mutually agreed-on focus of work and desired outcomes					
d.	Collect, organize, and interpret client data					
e.	Assess client strengths and limitations					
f.	Develop mutually agreed-on intervention goals and objectives					
g.	Select appropriate intervention strategies					
h.	Initiate actions to achieve organizational goals					
i.	Implement prevention interventions that enhance client capacities					
j.	Help clients resolve problems					
k.	Negotiate, mediate, and advocate for clients					
l.	Facilitate transitions and endings					
m.	Critically analyze, monitor, and evaluate interventions					

Chapter 7: Sexual Orientation and Services to GLBT Individuals

Competencies/Practice Behaviors Exercise 7.1
Whatever You Wanted to Know About Sex

Focus Competencies or Practice Behaviors:
- EP 2.1.1b Practice personal reflection and self-correction to assure continual professional development
- EP 2.1.3a Distinguish, appraise, and integrate multiple sources of knowledge, including research-based knowledge and practice wisdom
- EP 2.1.7a Utilize conceptual frameworks to guide the processes of assessment, intervention, and evaluation

A. Brief Description
The purpose of this exercise is to provide you with accurate information about sexual questions you have.

B. Objectives
You will:
1. Become less inhibited about sexual questions.
2. Receive answers to your questions in regard to sex and sexuality.

C. Procedure
1. Write one or more questions that you personally would like answers to in regard to sex and sexuality. The writers of the questions will remain anonymous.
2. At the next class period the instructor will read the questions one by one and provide answers. At times discussions may ensue.

Competencies/Practice Behaviors Exercise 7.2
Same Sex Marriages

Focus Competencies or Practice Behaviors:
- EP 2.1.1b Practice personal reflection and self-correction to assure continual professional development
- EP 2.1.1c Attend to professional roles and boundaries
- EP 2.1.2a Recognize and manage personal values in a way that allows professional values to guide practice
- EP 2.1.2b Make ethical decisions by applying standards of the National Association of Social Workers Code of Ethics and, as applicable, of the International Federation of Social Workers/International Association of Schools of Social Work Ethics in Social Work, Statement of Principles
- EP 2.1.3a Distinguish, appraise, and integrate multiple sources of knowledge, including research-based knowledge and practice wisdom
- EP 2.1.4b Gain sufficient self-awareness to eliminate the influence of personal biases and values in working with diverse groups
- EP 2.1.7a Utilize conceptual frameworks to guide the processes of assessment, intervention, and evaluation

- EP 2.1.7b Critique and apply knowledge to understand person and environment
- EP 2.1.8a Analyze, formulate, and advocate for policies that advance social well-being

A. Brief Description

This exercise is designed to have students anonymously share their views about the merits and shortcomings of legalizing same sex marriages.

B. Objectives

You will:
1. Practice your writing skills.
2. Become more aware of your personal views regarding same-sex marriages.

C. Procedure
1. Write on a sheet of paper (without writing your name) your views on the merits and shortcomings of legalizing same sex marriages.
2. The instructor collects these papers, and then redistributes them to the students—with each student getting one that was written by someone else. Each student then reads the written response that she or he received. The instructor ends the exercise by leading a discussion of the views that are expressed.
3. Write a brief report regarding your discomfort or prejudiced attitudes, and whether you were aware of this prior to this exercise

Competencies/Practice Behaviors Exercise 7.3
Role Play—Values Clarification About Gays and Lesbians

Focus Competencies or Practice Behaviors:
- EP 2.1.1b Practice personal reflection and self-correction to assure continual professional development
- EP 2.1.1c Attend to professional roles and boundaries
- EP 2.1.1d Demonstrate professional demeanor in behavior, appearance, and communication
- EP 2.1.2a Recognize and manage personal values in a way that allows professional values to guide practice
- EP 2.1.2b Make ethical decisions by applying standards of the National Association of Social Workers Code of Ethics and, as applicable, of the International Federation of Social Workers/International Association of Schools of Social Work Ethics in Social Work, Statement of Principles
- EP 2.1.3c Demonstrate effective oral and written communication in working with individuals, families, groups, organizations, communities, and colleagues
- EP 2.1.4a Recognize the extent to which a culture's structures and values may oppress, marginalize, alienate, or create or enhance privilege and power
- EP 2.1.4b Gain sufficient self-awareness to eliminate the influence of personal biases and values in working with diverse groups
- EP 2.1.5a Understand forms and mechanisms of oppression and discrimination
- EP 2.1.6a Use practice experience to inform scientific inquiry
- EP 2.1.7a Utilize conceptual frameworks to guide the processes of assessment, intervention, and evaluation
- EP 2.1.7b Critique and apply knowledge to understand person and environment

A. Brief Description
The objectives of this role play are to have you confront your values about gays and lesbians and to have you become aware of the myths and facts that exist regarding gays and lesbians.

B. Objectives
You will:
1. Confront your discomfort in talking about sexual orientation.
2. Become aware of the myths and facts about gays and lesbians.

C. Procedure
1. Form groups of three to five people. One person will portray the daughter or son who is coming out to his or her family. The others will assume the roles of the mother, father, and other siblings.
2. Role play the situation. Be aware of your verbal and nonverbal communication as you assume your roles.
3. After the role play, discuss your discomfort or prejudiced attitudes, and whether you were aware of this prior to this exercise. The instructor may end the exercise by summarizing (from the text) the myths and facts that exist about gays and lesbians, and you should read about them on your own.

Chapter 7 Competencies/Practice Behaviors Exercises Assessment:

Name: _____ Date: _____
Supervisor's Name: _____

Focus Competencies/Practice Behaviors:
- EP 2.1.1b   Practice personal reflection and self-correction to assure continual professional development
- EP 2.1.1c   Attend to professional roles and boundaries
- EP 2.1.1d   Demonstrate professional demeanor in behavior, appearance, and communication
- EP 2.1.2a   Recognize and manage personal values in a way that allows professional values to guide practice
- EP 2.1.2b   Make ethical decisions by applying standards of the National Association of Social Workers Code of Ethics and, as applicable, of the International Federation of Social Workers/International Association of Schools of Social Work Ethics in Social Work, Statement of Principles
- EP 2.1.3a   Distinguish, appraise, and integrate multiple sources of knowledge, including research-based knowledge and practice wisdom
- EP 2.1.3c   Demonstrate effective oral and written communication in working with individuals, families, groups, organizations, communities, and colleagues
- EP 2.1.4a   Recognize the extent to which a culture's structures and values may oppress, marginalize, alienate, or create or enhance privilege and power
- EP 2.1.4b   Gain sufficient self-awareness to eliminate the influence of personal biases and values in working with diverse groups
- EP 2.1.5a   Understand forms and mechanisms of oppression and discrimination
- EP 2.1.6a   Use practice experience to inform scientific inquiry
- EP 2.1.7a   Utilize conceptual frameworks to guide the processes of assessment, intervention, and evaluation
- EP 2.1.7b   Critique and apply knowledge to understand person and environment
- EP 2.1.8a   Analyze, formulate, and advocate for policies that advance social well-being

Instructions:
A. Evaluate your work or your partner's work in the Focus Competencies/Practice Behaviors by completing the Competencies/Practice Behaviors Assessment form below
B. What other Competencies/Practice Behaviors did you use to complete these Exercises? Be sure to record them in your assessments

1.	I have attained this competency/practice behavior (in the range of 81 to 100%)
2.	I have largely attained this competency/practice behavior (in the range of 61 to 80%)
3.	I have partially attained this competency/practice behavior (in the range of 41 to 60%)
4.	I have made a little progress in attaining this competency/practice behavior (in the range of 21 to 40%)
5.	I have made almost no progress in attaining this competency/practice behavior (in the range of 0 to 20%)

EPAS 2008 Core Competencies & Core Practice Behaviors	Student Self Assessment						Evaluator Feedback
Student and Evaluator Assessment Scale and Comments	0	1	2	3	4	5	Agree/Disagree/Comments
EP 2.1.1 Identify as a Professional Social Worker and Conduct Oneself Accordingly:							
a. Advocate for client access to the services of social work							
b. Practice personal reflection and self-correction to assure continual professional development							
c. Attend to professional roles and boundaries							
d. Demonstrate professional demeanor in behavior, appearance, and communication							
e. Engage in career-long learning							
f. Use supervision and consultation							
EP 2.1.2 Apply Social Work Ethical Principles to Guide Professional Practice:							
a. Recognize and manage personal values in a way that allows professional values to guide practice							
b. Make ethical decisions by applying NASW Code of Ethics and, as applicable, of the IFSW/IASSW Ethics in Social Work, Statement of Principles							
c. Tolerate ambiguity in resolving ethical conflicts							
d. Apply strategies of ethical reasoning to arrive at principled decisions							
EP 2.1.3 Apply Critical Thinking to Inform and Communicate Professional Judgments:							
a. Distinguish, appraise, and integrate multiple sources of knowledge, including research-based knowledge and practice wisdom							
b. Analyze models of assessment, prevention, intervention, and evaluation							
c. Demonstrate effective oral and written communication in working with individuals, families, groups, organizations, communities, and colleagues							
EP 2.1.4 Engage Diversity and Difference in Practice:							
a. Recognize the extent to which a culture's structures and values may oppress, marginalize, alienate, or create or enhance privilege and power							
b. Gain sufficient self-awareness to eliminate the influence of personal biases and values in working with diverse groups							
c. Recognize and communicate their understanding of the importance of difference in shaping life experiences							
d. View themselves as learners and engage those with whom they work as informants							
EP 2.1.5 Advance Human Rights and Social and Economic Justice:							
a. Understand forms and mechanisms of oppression and discrimination							
b. Advocate for human rights and social and economic justice							
c. Engage in practices that advance social and economic justice							
EP 2.1.6 Engage in Research-Informed Practice and Practice-Informed Research:							
a. Use practice experience to inform scientific inquiry							
b. Use research evidence to inform practice							

EP 2.1.7 Apply Knowledge of Human Behavior and the Social Environment:						
a.	Utilize conceptual frameworks to guide the processes of assessment, intervention, and evaluation					
b.	Critique and apply knowledge to understand person and environment					
EP 2.1.8 Engage in Policy Practice to Advance Social and Economic Well-Being and to Deliver Effective Social Work Services:						
a.	Analyze, formulate, and advocate for policies that advance social well-being					
b.	Collaborate with colleagues and clients for effective policy action					
EP 2.1.9 Respond to Contexts that Shape Practice:						
a.	Continuously discover, appraise, and attend to changing locales, populations, scientific and technological developments, and emerging societal trends to provide relevant services					
b.	Provide leadership in promoting sustainable changes in service delivery and practice to improve the quality of social services					
EP 2.1.10 Engage, Assess, Intervene, and Evaluate with Individuals, Families, Groups, Organizations and Communities:						
a.	Substantively and affectively prepare for action with individuals, families, groups, organizations, and communities					
b.	Use empathy and other interpersonal skills					
c.	Develop a mutually agreed-on focus of work and desired outcomes					
d.	Collect, organize, and interpret client data					
e.	Assess client strengths and limitations					
f.	Develop mutually agreed-on intervention goals and objectives					
g.	Select appropriate intervention strategies					
h.	Initiate actions to achieve organizational goals					
i.	Implement prevention interventions that enhance client capacities					
j.	Help clients resolve problems					
k.	Negotiate, mediate, and advocate for clients					
l.	Facilitate transitions and endings					
m.	Critically analyze, monitor, and evaluate interventions					

Chapter 8: Drug Abuse and Drug Treatment Programs

Competencies/Practice Behaviors Exercise 8.1
Everything You Wanted to Know About Drug Use and Abuse

Focus Competencies or Practice Behaviors:
- EP 2.1.3a   Distinguish, appraise, and integrate multiple sources of knowledge, including research-based knowledge and practice wisdom
- EP 2.1.7a   Utilize conceptual frameworks to guide the processes of assessment, intervention, and evaluation
- EP 2.1.7b   Critique and apply knowledge to understand person and environment
- EP 2.1.9a   Continuously discover, appraise, and attend to changing locales, populations, scientific and technological developments, and emerging societal trends to provide relevant services
- EP 2.1.10a   Substantively and affectively prepare for action with individuals, families, groups, organizations, and communities

A.   Brief Description
     This exercise is designed to answer your questions about drug use and drug abuse.

B.   Objectives
     You will:
     1.   Become more familiar with drug use and the effects of drugs.
     2.   Practice your writing skills.

C.   Procedure
     1.   Write one or two questions you have about drug use or abuse. Possible focuses of such questions include (a) adverse effects of certain drugs, (b) how to get someone to acknowledge that he or she has a drug problem, and (c) what a person can do if one of his or her parents or a roommate has a serious drug problem but denies that a problem exists. The writers of the questions will remain anonymous.
     2.   Prior to the next class period the instructor will endeavor to obtain answers to the questions raised.
     3.   At the next class period the instructor will provide answers to the questions, one by one.

Competencies/Practice Behaviors Exercise 8.2
Role Play—Saying "No" to a Drink

Focus Competencies or Practice Behaviors:
- EP 2.1.1b   Practice personal reflection and self-correction to assure continual professional development
- EP 2.1.2a   Recognize and manage personal values in a way that allows professional values to guide practice
- EP 2.1.4a   Recognize the extent to which a culture's structures and values may oppress, marginalize, alienate, or create or enhance privilege and power

- EP 2.1.9a   Continuously discover, appraise, and attend to changing locales, populations, scientific and technological developments, and emerging societal trends to provide relevant services
- EP 2.1.10a Substantively and affectively prepare for action with individuals, families, groups, organizations, and communities

A. Brief Description
   The purpose of this exercise is to demonstrate how to assertively refuse a drink.

B. Objectives
   You will:
   1. Practice assertiveness.
   2. Practice role playing possible situations in which you would feel pressure to drink.

C. Procedure
   1. Many of you have difficulty knowing what to say when a friend or a group of friends puts pressure on you to have a drink or another drink when you do not want one. Ask a friend or classmate to role-play a situation in which one person pressures another to take a drink and the other person seeks to respond assertively that she or he does not want a drink. Then you should switch roles and perform the role-play once again.
   2. Write a brief report discussing the merits and shortcomings of the role attempts to say "No" assertively.

Competencies/Practice Behaviors Exercise 8.3
Role Play—Motivational Interviewing

Focus Competencies or Practice Behaviors:
- EP 2.1.1b   Practice personal reflection and self-correction to assure continual professional development
- EP 2.1.1d   Demonstrate professional demeanor in behavior, appearance, and communication
- EP 2.1.3b   Analyze models of assessment, prevention, intervention, and evaluation
- EP 2.1.3c   Demonstrate effective oral and written communication in working with individuals, families, groups, organizations, communities, and colleagues
- EP 2.1.4c   Recognize and communicate their understanding of the importance of difference in shaping life experiences
- EP 2.1.7a   Utilize conceptual frameworks to guide the processes of assessment, intervention, and evaluation
- EP 2.1.10a Substantively and affectively prepare for action with individuals, families, groups, organizations, and communities
- EP 2.1.10b Use empathy and other interpersonal skills
- EP 2.1.10j Help clients resolve problems
- EP 2.1.10m Critically analyze, monitor, and evaluate interventions

A. Brief Description
   The purpose of this role play is to practice motivational interviewing.

B. Objectives
   You will:
   1. Practice your interviewing skills.
   2. Evaluate the effectiveness of motivational interviewing.

C. Procedure
  1. Read the material in the text regarding motivational interviewing, including the following fundamentals
     a. Express empathy
     b. Support self-efficacy
     c. Roll with resistance
     d. Develop discrepancy
  2. The instructor will portray the social worker in a role play with a student volunteer portraying a client resistant to change.
  3. Each student will practice motivational interviewing with the classmate beside him or her. Each will portray the social worker and then switch to play the client.
  4. Discuss the pros and cons you find with motivational interviewing.

Chapter 8 Competencies/Practice Behaviors Exercises Assessment:

Name: _____ **Date:** _____
Supervisor's Name: _____

Focus Competencies/Practice Behaviors:
- EP 2.1.1b   Practice personal reflection and self-correction to assure continual professional development
- EP 2.1.1d   Demonstrate professional demeanor in behavior, appearance, and communication
- EP 2.1.2a   Recognize and manage personal values in a way that allows professional values to guide practice
- EP 2.1.3a   Distinguish, appraise, and integrate multiple sources of knowledge, including research-based knowledge and practice wisdom
- EP 2.1.3b   Analyze models of assessment, prevention, intervention, and evaluation
- EP 2.1.3c   Demonstrate effective oral and written communication in working with individuals, families, groups, organizations, communities, and colleagues
- EP 2.1.4a   Recognize the extent to which a culture's structures and values may oppress, marginalize, alienate, or create or enhance privilege and power
- EP 2.1.4c   Recognize and communicate their understanding of the importance of difference in shaping life experiences
- EP 2.1.7a   Utilize conceptual frameworks to guide the processes of assessment, intervention, and evaluation
- EP 2.1.7b   Critique and apply knowledge to understand person and environment
- EP 2.1.9a   Continuously discover, appraise, and attend to changing locales, populations, scientific and technological developments, and emerging societal trends to provide relevant services
- EP 2.1.10a   Substantively and affectively prepare for action with individuals, families, groups, organizations, and communities
- EP 2.1.10b   Use empathy and other interpersonal skills
- EP 2.1.10j   Help clients resolve problems
- EP 2.1.10m   Critically analyze, monitor, and evaluate interventions

Instructions:
A.   Evaluate your work or your partner's work in the Focus Competencies/Practice Behaviors by completing the Competencies/Practice Behaviors Assessment form below
B.   What other Competencies/Practice Behaviors did you use to complete these Exercises? Be sure to record them in your assessments

1.	I have attained this competency/practice behavior (in the range of 81 to 100%)
2.	I have largely attained this competency/practice behavior (in the range of 61 to 80%)
3.	I have partially attained this competency/practice behavior (in the range of 41 to 60%)
4.	I have made a little progress in attaining this competency/practice behavior (in the range of 21 to 40%)
5.	I have made almost no progress in attaining this competency/practice behavior (in the range of 0 to 20%)

EPAS 2008 Core Competencies & Core Practice Behaviors	Student Self Assessment						Evaluator Feedback
Student and Evaluator Assessment Scale and Comments	0	1	2	3	4	5	Agree/Disagree/Comments
EP 2.1.1 Identify as a Professional Social Worker and Conduct Oneself Accordingly:							
a. Advocate for client access to the services of social work							
b. Practice personal reflection and self-correction to assure continual professional development							
c. Attend to professional roles and boundaries							
d. Demonstrate professional demeanor in behavior, appearance, and communication							
e. Engage in career-long learning							
f. Use supervision and consultation							
EP 2.1.2 Apply Social Work Ethical Principles to Guide Professional Practice:							
a. Recognize and manage personal values in a way that allows professional values to guide practice							
b. Make ethical decisions by applying NASW Code of Ethics and, as applicable, of the IFSW/IASSW Ethics in Social Work, Statement of Principles							
c. Tolerate ambiguity in resolving ethical conflicts							
d. Apply strategies of ethical reasoning to arrive at principled decisions							
EP 2.1.3 Apply Critical Thinking to Inform and Communicate Professional Judgments:							
a. Distinguish, appraise, and integrate multiple sources of knowledge, including research-based knowledge and practice wisdom							
b. Analyze models of assessment, prevention, intervention, and evaluation							
c. Demonstrate effective oral and written communication in working with individuals, families, groups, organizations, communities, and colleagues							
EP 2.1.4 Engage Diversity and Difference in Practice:							
a. Recognize the extent to which a culture's structures and values may oppress, marginalize, alienate, or create or enhance privilege and power							
b. Gain sufficient self-awareness to eliminate the influence of personal biases and values in working with diverse groups							
c. Recognize and communicate their understanding of the importance of difference in shaping life experiences							
d. View themselves as learners and engage those with whom they work as informants							
EP 2.1.5 Advance Human Rights and Social and Economic Justice:							
a. Understand forms and mechanisms of oppression and discrimination							
b. Advocate for human rights and social and economic justice							
c. Engage in practices that advance social and economic justice							
EP 2.1.6 Engage in Research-Informed Practice and Practice-Informed Research:							
a. Use practice experience to inform scientific inquiry							
b. Use research evidence to inform practice							

EP 2.1.7 Apply Knowledge of Human Behavior and the Social Environment:							
a.	Utilize conceptual frameworks to guide the processes of assessment, intervention, and evaluation						
b.	Critique and apply knowledge to understand person and environment						
EP 2.1.8 Engage in Policy Practice to Advance Social and Economic Well-Being and to Deliver Effective Social Work Services:							
a.	Analyze, formulate, and advocate for policies that advance social well-being						
b.	Collaborate with colleagues and clients for effective policy action						
EP 2.1.9 Respond to Contexts that Shape Practice:							
a.	Continuously discover, appraise, and attend to changing locales, populations, scientific and technological developments, and emerging societal trends to provide relevant services						
b.	Provide leadership in promoting sustainable changes in service delivery and practice to improve the quality of social services						
EP 2.1.10 Engage, Assess, Intervene, and Evaluate with Individuals, Families, Groups, Organizations and Communities:							
a.	Substantively and affectively prepare for action with individuals, families, groups, organizations, and communities						
b.	Use empathy and other interpersonal skills						
c.	Develop a mutually agreed-on focus of work and desired outcomes						
d.	Collect, organize, and interpret client data						
e.	Assess client strengths and limitations						
f.	Develop mutually agreed-on intervention goals and objectives						
g.	Select appropriate intervention strategies						
h.	Initiate actions to achieve organizational goals						
i.	Implement prevention interventions that enhance client capacities						
j.	Help clients resolve problems						
k.	Negotiate, mediate, and advocate for clients						
l.	Facilitate transitions and endings						
m.	Critically analyze, monitor, and evaluate interventions						

Chapter 9: Crime, Juvenile Delinquency, and Correctional Services

Competencies/Practice Behaviors Exercise 9.1
Improving the Correctional System

Focus Competencies or Practice Behaviors:
- EP 2.1.3b   Analyze models of assessment, prevention, intervention, and evaluation
- EP 2.1.3c   Demonstrate effective oral and written communication in working with individuals, families, groups, organizations, communities, and colleagues
- EP 2.1.4b   Gain sufficient self-awareness to eliminate the influence of personal biases and values in working with diverse groups
- EP 2.1.4c   Recognize and communicate their understanding of the importance of difference in shaping life experiences
- EP 2.1.6b   Use research evidence to inform practice
- EP 2.1.7a   Utilize conceptual frameworks to guide the processes of assessment, intervention, and evaluation
- EP 2.1.7b   Critique and apply knowledge to understand person and environment
- EP 2.1.8a   Analyze, formulate, and advocate for policies that advance social well-being
- EP 2.1.10a   Substantively and affectively prepare for action with individuals, families, groups, organizations, and communities

A. Brief Description
    This exercise is designed to increase your understanding of alternatives for making the correctional system more effective in curbing criminal behavior.

B. Objectives
    You will:
    1. Learn about the correctional system.
    2. Increase your confidence in public speaking.

C. Procedure
    1. Read the following:

> This is an opportunity for you to come up with a design for a correctional system that will be more effective in curbing criminal behavior than our present prison system. The present prison system is both costly and ineffective in curbing criminal behavior. It costs over $35,000 of taxpayers' money per inmate per year to lock up criminal offenders. Yet, an estimated half of the inmates who return to society are, within a few years, found guilty of another crime and sent back to prison. I want you to develop a correctional system that is (a) humane, (b) more effective in curbing criminal activity than the prison system, and (c) no more costly than $35,000 per inmate per year. Creativity is encouraged. On a separate page cite the merits and shortcomings of your proposal.

2. You will present your proposal to the class, (excluding the merits and shortcomings page you wrote) and they will discuss the merits and the shortcomings of each proposal. Compare your ideas of merits and shortcomings of your proposal with the responses from the class.
3. You will be asked which of the suggested proposals appear likely to be more effective in curbing criminal activity than the current penal system.

Competencies/Practice Behaviors Exercise 9.2
A Day in Prison

Focus Competencies or Practice Behaviors:
- EP 2.1.1b Practice personal reflection and self-correction to assure continual professional development
- EP 2.1.4a Recognize the extent to which a culture's structures and values may oppress, marginalize, alienate, or create or enhance privilege and power
- EP 2.1.4d View themselves as learners and engage those with whom they work as informants
- EP 2.1.5a Understand forms and mechanisms of oppression and discrimination
- EP 2.1.7a Utilize conceptual frameworks to guide the processes of assessment, intervention, and evaluation
- EP 2.1.7b Critique and apply knowledge to understand person and environment
- EP 2.1.9a Continuously discover, appraise, and attend to changing locales, populations, scientific and technological developments, and emerging societal trends to provide relevant services
- EP 2.1.10a Substantively and affectively prepare for action with individuals, families, groups, organizations, and communities

A. Brief Description
This exercise is designed to give you an understanding, and a feeling, of what it is like to be in a correctional facility.

B. Objectives
You will:
1. Become more aware of correctional facilities.
2. Practice your writing skills.

C. Procedure
1. Visit a nearby correctional facility, such as a jail, prison, or correctional school, and discuss with the staff—and, if possible, the inmates (or residents)—what life is like in such a facility. If inmates or residents become involved in a question-and-answer session with you, you should ask any pertinent questions you desire, with the understanding that the residents have the right to refuse to answer any questions they consider to be too personal.
2. Write a report discussing your thoughts and feelings about this visit to a correctional facility.

Competencies/Practice Behaviors Exercise 9.3
Role Play—Approaches for Increasing or Decreasing Sentences

Focus Competencies or Practice Behaviors:

- EP 2.1.1b   Practice personal reflection and self-correction to assure continual professional development
- EP 2.1.1c   Attend to professional roles and boundaries
- EP 2.1.1d   Demonstrate professional demeanor in behavior, appearance, and communication
- EP 2.1.2a   Recognize and manage personal values in a way that allows professional values to guide practice
- EP 2.1.2b   Make ethical decisions by applying standards of the National Association of Social Workers Code of Ethics and, as applicable, of the International Federation of Social Workers/International Association of Schools of Social Work Ethics in Social Work, Statement of Principles
- EP 2.1.2c   Tolerate ambiguity in resolving ethical conflicts
- EP 2.1.2d   Apply strategies of ethical reasoning to arrive at principled decisions
- EP 2.1.3a   Distinguish, appraise, and integrate multiple sources of knowledge, including research-based knowledge and practice wisdom
- EP 2.1.3b   Analyze models of assessment, prevention, intervention, and evaluation
- EP 2.1.3c   Demonstrate effective oral and written communication in working with individuals, families, groups, organizations, communities, and colleagues
- EP 2.1.4a   Recognize the extent to which a culture's structures and values may oppress, marginalize, alienate, or create or enhance privilege and power
- EP 2.1.4b   Gain sufficient self-awareness to eliminate the influence of personal biases and values in working with diverse groups
- EP 2.1.4c   Recognize and communicate their understanding of the importance of difference in shaping life experiences
- EP 2.1.5a   Understand forms and mechanisms of oppression and discrimination
- EP 2.1.6b   Use research evidence to inform practice
- EP 2.1.7a   Utilize conceptual frameworks to guide the processes of assessment, intervention, and evaluation
- EP 2.1.7b   Critique and apply knowledge to understand person and environment
- EP 2.1.8a   Analyze, formulate, and advocate for policies that advance social well-being
- EP 2.1.10a   Substantively and affectively prepare for action with individuals, families, groups, organizations, and communities

A. Brief Description
This exercise is designed to increase your understanding of the appropriateness of various sentences for the crimes committed.

B. Objectives
You will:
1. Research the following approaches that were cited in the text.
2. Increase your public speaking skills.

C. Procedure
1. You will be assigned the role of debating for or against one of the following approaches to changing the sentencing guidelines.
2. Research articles and opinions regarding your assigned approach and be prepared to debate at the next class period.

3. Students who have been assigned the pro aspect of each approach will begin the role play by presenting their opinions; the students assigned the con aspect of this approach will then present their findings.
4. The rebuttal of each will be allowed to proceed and the debate will continue for 15 minutes.
5. Another approach will begin and proceed in the same manner, and continue until all the following approaches have been discussed.

a.	Instituting swift and certain punishment
b.	Imposing harsher sentences
c.	Separating repeat offenders from society
d.	Getting tougher on white-collar crime
e.	Creating uniform sentences
f.	Decriminalizing public-order offenses
g.	Imposing stricter gun control

Chapter 9 Competencies/Practice Behaviors Exercises Assessment:

Name: _____ **Date:** _____
Supervisor's Name: _____

Focus Competencies/Practice Behaviors:
- EP 2.1.1b Practice personal reflection and self-correction to assure continual professional development
- EP 2.1.1c Attend to professional roles and boundaries
- EP 2.1.1d Demonstrate professional demeanor in behavior, appearance, and communication
- EP 2.1.2a Recognize and manage personal values in a way that allows professional values to guide practice
- EP 2.1.2b Make ethical decisions by applying standards of the National Association of Social Workers Code of Ethics and, as applicable, of the International Federation of Social Workers/International Association of Schools of Social Work Ethics in Social Work, Statement of Principles
- EP 2.1.2c Tolerate ambiguity in resolving ethical conflicts
- EP 2.1.2d Apply strategies of ethical reasoning to arrive at principled decisions
- EP 2.1.3a Distinguish, appraise, and integrate multiple sources of knowledge, including research-based knowledge and practice wisdom
- EP 2.1.3b Analyze models of assessment, prevention, intervention, and evaluation
- EP 2.1.3c Demonstrate effective oral and written communication in working with individuals, families, groups, organizations, communities, and colleagues
- EP 2.1.4a Recognize the extent to which a culture's structures and values may oppress, marginalize, alienate, or create or enhance privilege and power
- EP 2.1.4b Gain sufficient self-awareness to eliminate the influence of personal biases and values in working with diverse groups
- EP 2.1.4c Recognize and communicate their understanding of the importance of difference in shaping life experiences
- EP 2.1.4d View themselves as learners and engage those with whom they work as informants
- EP 2.1.5a Understand forms and mechanisms of oppression and discrimination
- EP 2.1.6b Use research evidence to inform practice
- EP 2.1.7a Utilize conceptual frameworks to guide the processes of assessment, intervention, and evaluation
- EP 2.1.7b Critique and apply knowledge to understand person and environment
- EP 2.1.8a Analyze, formulate, and advocate for policies that advance social well-being
- EP 2.1.9a Continuously discover, appraise, and attend to changing locales, populations, scientific and technological developments, and emerging societal trends to provide relevant services
- EP 2.1.10a Substantively and affectively prepare for action with individuals, families, groups, organizations, and communities

Instructions:
A.   Evaluate your work or your partner's work in the Focus Competencies/Practice Behaviors by completing the Competencies/Practice Behaviors Assessment form below
B.   What other Competencies/Practice Behaviors did you use to complete these Exercises? Be sure to record them in your assessments

1.	I have attained this competency/practice behavior (in the range of 81 to 100%)
2.	I have largely attained this competency/practice behavior (in the range of 61 to 80%)
3.	I have partially attained this competency/practice behavior (in the range of 41 to 60%)
4.	I have made a little progress in attaining this competency/practice behavior (in the range of 21 to 40%)
5.	I have made almost no progress in attaining this competency/practice behavior (in the range of 0 to 20%)

EPAS 2008 Core Competencies & Core Practice Behaviors	Student Self Assessment						Evaluator Feedback
Student and Evaluator Assessment Scale and Comments	0	1	2	3	4	5	Agree/Disagree/Comments
EP 2.1.1 Identify as a Professional Social Worker and Conduct Oneself Accordingly:							
a. Advocate for client access to the services of social work							
b. Practice personal reflection and self-correction to assure continual professional development							
c. Attend to professional roles and boundaries							
d. Demonstrate professional demeanor in behavior, appearance, and communication							
e. Engage in career-long learning							
f. Use supervision and consultation							
EP 2.1.2 Apply Social Work Ethical Principles to Guide Professional Practice:							
a. Recognize and manage personal values in a way that allows professional values to guide practice							
b. Make ethical decisions by applying NASW Code of Ethics and, as applicable, of the IFSW/IASSW Ethics in Social Work, Statement of Principles							
c. Tolerate ambiguity in resolving ethical conflicts							
d. Apply strategies of ethical reasoning to arrive at principled decisions							
EP 2.1.3 Apply Critical Thinking to Inform and Communicate Professional Judgments:							
a. Distinguish, appraise, and integrate multiple sources of knowledge, including research-based knowledge and practice wisdom							
b. Analyze models of assessment, prevention, intervention, and evaluation							
c. Demonstrate effective oral and written communication in working with individuals, families, groups, organizations, communities, and colleagues							
EP 2.1.4 Engage Diversity and Difference in Practice:							
a. Recognize the extent to which a culture's structures and values may oppress, marginalize, alienate, or create or enhance privilege and power							
b. Gain sufficient self-awareness to eliminate the influence of personal biases and values in working with diverse groups							
c. Recognize and communicate their understanding of the importance of difference in shaping life experiences							
d. View themselves as learners and engage those with whom they work as informants							
EP 2.1.5 Advance Human Rights and Social and Economic Justice:							
a. Understand forms and mechanisms of oppression and discrimination							
b. Advocate for human rights and social and economic justice							
c. Engage in practices that advance social and economic justice							

EP 2.1.6 Engage in Research-Informed Practice and Practice-Informed Research:							
a.	Use practice experience to inform scientific inquiry						
b.	Use research evidence to inform practice						
EP 2.1.7 Apply Knowledge of Human Behavior and the Social Environment:							
a.	Utilize conceptual frameworks to guide the processes of assessment, intervention, and evaluation						
b.	Critique and apply knowledge to understand person and environment						
EP 2.1.8 Engage in Policy Practice to Advance Social and Economic Well-Being and to Deliver Effective Social Work Services:							
a.	Analyze, formulate, and advocate for policies that advance social well-being						
b.	Collaborate with colleagues and clients for effective policy action						
EP 2.1.9 Respond to Contexts that Shape Practice:							
a.	Continuously discover, appraise, and attend to changing locales, populations, scientific and technological developments, and emerging societal trends to provide relevant services						
b.	Provide leadership in promoting sustainable changes in service delivery and practice to improve the quality of social services						
EP 2.1.10 Engage, Assess, Intervene, and Evaluate with Individuals, Families, Groups, Organizations and Communities:							
a.	Substantively and affectively prepare for action with individuals, families, groups, organizations, and communities						
b.	Use empathy and other interpersonal skills						
c.	Develop a mutually agreed-on focus of work and desired outcomes						
d.	Collect, organize, and interpret client data						
e.	Assess client strengths and limitations						
f.	Develop mutually agreed-on intervention goals and objectives						
g.	Select appropriate intervention strategies						
h.	Initiate actions to achieve organizational goals						
i.	Implement prevention interventions that enhance client capacities						
j.	Help clients resolve problems						
k.	Negotiate, mediate, and advocate for clients						
l.	Facilitate transitions and endings						
m.	Critically analyze, monitor, and evaluate interventions						

Chapter 10: Problems in Education and School Social Work

Competencies/Practice Behaviors Exercise 10.1
Problems in My High School

Focus Competencies or Practice Behaviors:
- EP 2.1.3a   Distinguish, appraise, and integrate multiple sources of knowledge, including research-based knowledge and practice wisdom
- EP 2.1.3c   Demonstrate effective oral and written communication in working with individuals, families, groups, organizations, communities, and colleagues
- EP 2.1.7a   Utilize conceptual frameworks to guide the processes of assessment, intervention, and evaluation
- EP 2.1.7b   Critique and apply knowledge to understand person and environment
- EP 2.1.8a   Analyze, formulate, and advocate for policies that advance social well-being
- EP 2.1.9a   Continuously discover, appraise, and attend to changing locales, populations, scientific and technological developments, and emerging societal trends to provide relevant services
- EP 2.1.10a Substantively and affectively prepare for action with individuals, families, groups, organizations, and communities

A. Brief Description
   This exercise is designed to help you become more aware of how the major problems in your high schools can be combated.

B. Objectives
   You will:
   1. Learn about various problems in education and explore the field of school social work.
   2. Practice critical thinking and your writing skills.

C. Procedure
   1. Think back to your high school days and write down on a sheet of paper answers to the following question: What do you see as the three major problem areas that need attention in order to improve the level of education at your high school?
   2. Write a proposal discussing what needs to be done to combat these problems and deliver it to the instructor.
   3. The instructor will ask a few students to share, with the entire class, the problem area they identified, particularly those problems that are serious and appear to be extremely difficult to resolve, and the proposal that was suggested to alleviate those problems.

Competencies/Practice Behaviors Exercise 10.2
Role Play—Bullying and Cyberbullying

Focus Competencies or Practice Behaviors:
- EP 2.1.1b   Practice personal reflection and self-correction to assure continual professional development
- EP 2.1.1c   Attend to professional roles and boundaries

- EP 2.1.1d Demonstrate professional demeanor in behavior, appearance, and communication
- EP 2.1.2c Tolerate ambiguity in resolving ethical conflicts
- EP 2.1.2d Apply strategies of ethical reasoning to arrive at principled decisions
- EP 2.1.3a Distinguish, appraise, and integrate multiple sources of knowledge, including research-based knowledge and practice wisdom
- EP 2.1.3c Demonstrate effective oral and written communication in working with individuals, families, groups, organizations, communities, and colleagues
- EP 2.1.4a Recognize the extent to which a culture's structures and values may oppress, marginalize, alienate, or create or enhance privilege and power
- EP 2.1.4b Gain sufficient self-awareness to eliminate the influence of personal biases and values in working with diverse groups
- EP 2.1.4c Recognize and communicate their understanding of the importance of difference in shaping life experiences
- EP 2.1.5a Understand forms and mechanisms of oppression and discrimination
- EP 2.1.7a Utilize conceptual frameworks to guide the processes of assessment, intervention, and evaluation
- EP 2.1.7b Critique and apply knowledge to understand person and environment
- EP 2.1.8a Analyze, formulate, and advocate for policies that advance social well-being
- EP 2.1.8b Collaborate with colleagues and clients for effective policy action
- EP 2.1.9a Continuously discover, appraise, and attend to changing locales, populations, scientific and technological developments, and emerging societal trends to provide relevant services
- EP 2.1.10a Substantively and affectively prepare for action with individuals, families, groups, organizations, and communities
- EP 2.1.10b Use empathy and other interpersonal skills
- EP 2.1.10f Develop mutually agreed-on intervention goals and objectives
- EP 2.1.10j Help clients resolve problems

A. Brief Description

This role play is designed to help you become more aware of the problem of bullying and cyberbullying in our schools and deciding how to combat this problem.

B. Objectives
You will:
1. Role play a situation in which a family is called into a meeting with school personnel regarding the child's constant bullying behavior.
2. Better understand the role of school social workers.

C. Procedure
1. Read the vignette below.
2. Form groups of four or five each. Each person will be assigned one of the roles from the vignette.
3. The role play will proceed as if this was the first meeting after Carlton was suspended for bullying.

> Vignette:
>
> **Carlton**—is a 13-year-old boy who is big for his age and is considered the worst bully in the school. He has been in several physical fights, as well as verbal abuse of most of the girls in the school. He uses foul language and demeaning sexual terms. He has been warned many times and after this last fight, his victim was admitted to the hospital for a broken arm. The school suspended Carlton, with the possibility of expulsion pending.
>
> **Mrs. LeBeau**—is Carlton's mom, who is trying to make a home for Carlton and his three younger siblings. The father is out of the picture and has been since the last baby was born. Marcella is trying to work two jobs, plus take care of the three babies at home. Carlton is usually left to babysit after school.
>
> **Ms. Aquilara**—is the school social worker, who is very familiar with Carlton. She has called this meeting to try to prevent Carlton's expulsion and to devise a plan to alleviate his bullying.
>
> **Mr. Stonewall**—is the school principal and would like nothing better than to have Carlton expelled. This will set an example for any other kids who think they can bully others and get away with it.
>
> **Ms. Stuwitch**—is the lawyer representing the family of the student who was taken to the hospital with a broken arm. Her only reason for being in this meeting is to get her "pound of flesh" for the family she represents. She could care less about Carlton or his situation.

4. Try to come to some understanding within this group as to what can be done to keep Carlton in school and modify his behavior, while appeasing the others at this meeting.

Chapter 10 Competencies/Practice Behaviors Exercises Assessment:

Name: _____ Date: _____
Supervisor's Name: _____

Focus Competencies/Practice Behaviors:
- EP 2.1.1b   Practice personal reflection and self-correction to assure continual professional development
- EP 2.1.1c   Attend to professional roles and boundaries
- EP 2.1.1d   Demonstrate professional demeanor in behavior, appearance, and communication
- EP 2.1.2c   Tolerate ambiguity in resolving ethical conflicts
- EP 2.1.2d   Apply strategies of ethical reasoning to arrive at principled decisions
- EP 2.1.3a   Distinguish, appraise, and integrate multiple sources of knowledge, including research-based knowledge and practice wisdom
- EP 2.1.3c   Demonstrate effective oral and written communication in working with individuals, families, groups, organizations, communities, and colleagues
- EP 2.1.4a   Recognize the extent to which a culture's structures and values may oppress, marginalize, alienate, or create or enhance privilege and power
- EP 2.1.4b   Gain sufficient self-awareness to eliminate the influence of personal biases and values in working with diverse groups
- EP 2.1.4c   Recognize and communicate their understanding of the importance of difference in shaping life experiences
- EP 2.1.5a   Understand forms and mechanisms of oppression and discrimination
- EP 2.1.7a   Utilize conceptual frameworks to guide the processes of assessment, intervention, and evaluation
- EP 2.1.7b   Critique and apply knowledge to understand person and environment
- EP 2.1.8a   Analyze, formulate, and advocate for policies that advance social well-being
- EP 2.1.8b   Collaborate with colleagues and clients for effective policy action
- EP 2.1.9a   Continuously discover, appraise, and attend to changing locales, populations, scientific and technological developments, and emerging societal trends to provide relevant services
- EP 2.1.10a   Substantively and affectively prepare for action with individuals, families, groups, organizations, and communities
- EP 2.1.10b   Use empathy and other interpersonal skills
- EP 2.1.10f   Develop mutually agreed-on intervention goals and objectives
- EP 2.1.10j   Help clients resolve problems

Instructions:
A.   Evaluate your work or your partner's work in the Focus Competencies/Practice Behaviors by completing the Competencies/Practice Behaviors Assessment form below
B.   What other Competencies/Practice Behaviors did you use to complete these Exercises? Be sure to record them in your assessments

1.	I have attained this competency/practice behavior (in the range of 81 to 100%)
2.	I have largely attained this competency/practice behavior (in the range of 61 to 80%)
3.	I have partially attained this competency/practice behavior (in the range of 41 to 60%)
4.	I have made a little progress in attaining this competency/practice behavior (in the range of 21 to 40%)
5.	I have made almost no progress in attaining this competency/practice behavior (in the range of 0 to 20%)

EPAS 2008 Core Competencies & Core Practice Behaviors	Student Self Assessment						Evaluator Feedback
Student and Evaluator Assessment Scale and Comments	0	1	2	3	4	5	Agree/Disagree/Comments
EP 2.1.1 Identify as a Professional Social Worker and Conduct Oneself Accordingly:							
a. Advocate for client access to the services of social work							
b. Practice personal reflection and self-correction to assure continual professional development							
c. Attend to professional roles and boundaries							
d. Demonstrate professional demeanor in behavior, appearance, and communication							
e. Engage in career-long learning							
f. Use supervision and consultation							
EP 2.1.2 Apply Social Work Ethical Principles to Guide Professional Practice:							
a. Recognize and manage personal values in a way that allows professional values to guide practice							
b. Make ethical decisions by applying NASW Code of Ethics and, as applicable, of the IFSW/IASSW Ethics in Social Work, Statement of Principles							
c. Tolerate ambiguity in resolving ethical conflicts							
d. Apply strategies of ethical reasoning to arrive at principled decisions							
EP 2.1.3 Apply Critical Thinking to Inform and Communicate Professional Judgments:							
a. Distinguish, appraise, and integrate multiple sources of knowledge, including research-based knowledge and practice wisdom							
b. Analyze models of assessment, prevention, intervention, and evaluation							
c. Demonstrate effective oral and written communication in working with individuals, families, groups, organizations, communities, and colleagues							
EP 2.1.4 Engage Diversity and Difference in Practice:							
a. Recognize the extent to which a culture's structures and values may oppress, marginalize, alienate, or create or enhance privilege and power							
b. Gain sufficient self-awareness to eliminate the influence of personal biases and values in working with diverse groups							
c. Recognize and communicate their understanding of the importance of difference in shaping life experiences							
d. View themselves as learners and engage those with whom they work as informants							
EP 2.1.5 Advance Human Rights and Social and Economic Justice:							
a. Understand forms and mechanisms of oppression and discrimination							
b. Advocate for human rights and social and economic justice							
c. Engage in practices that advance social and economic justice							
EP 2.1.6 Engage in Research-Informed Practice and Practice-Informed Research:							
a. Use practice experience to inform scientific inquiry							
b. Use research evidence to inform practice							

EP 2.1.7 Apply Knowledge of Human Behavior and the Social Environment:						
a.	Utilize conceptual frameworks to guide the processes of assessment, intervention, and evaluation					
b.	Critique and apply knowledge to understand person and environment					
EP 2.1.8 Engage in Policy Practice to Advance Social and Economic Well-Being and to Deliver Effective Social Work Services:						
a.	Analyze, formulate, and advocate for policies that advance social well-being					
b.	Collaborate with colleagues and clients for effective policy action					
EP 2.1.9 Respond to Contexts that Shape Practice:						
a.	Continuously discover, appraise, and attend to changing locales, populations, scientific and technological developments, and emerging societal trends to provide relevant services					
b.	Provide leadership in promoting sustainable changes in service delivery and practice to improve the quality of social services					
EP 2.1.10 Engage, Assess, Intervene, and Evaluate with Individuals, Families, Groups, Organizations and Communities:						
a.	Substantively and affectively prepare for action with individuals, families, groups, organizations, and communities					
b.	Use empathy and other interpersonal skills					
c.	Develop a mutually agreed-on focus of work and desired outcomes					
d.	Collect, organize, and interpret client data					
e.	Assess client strengths and limitations					
f.	Develop mutually agreed-on intervention goals and objectives					
g.	Select appropriate intervention strategies					
h.	Initiate actions to achieve organizational goals					
i.	Implement prevention interventions that enhance client capacities					
j.	Help clients resolve problems					
k.	Negotiate, mediate, and advocate for clients					
l.	Facilitate transitions and endings					
m.	Critically analyze, monitor, and evaluate interventions					

Chapter 11: Work-Related Problems and Social Work in the Workplace

Competencies/Practice Behaviors Exercise 11.1
Services That Should Be Provided by Social Workers in the Workplace

Focus Competencies or Practice Behaviors:
- EP 2.1.3a   Distinguish, appraise, and integrate multiple sources of knowledge, including research-based knowledge and practice wisdom
- EP 2.1.3c   Demonstrate effective oral and written communication in working with individuals, families, groups, organizations, communities, and colleagues
- EP 2.1.7a   Utilize conceptual frameworks to guide the processes of assessment, intervention, and evaluation
- EP 2.1.7b   Critique and apply knowledge to understand person and environment
- EP 2.1.9a   Continuously discover, appraise, and attend to changing locales, populations, scientific and technological developments, and emerging societal trends to provide relevant services
- EP 2.1.10a   Substantively and affectively prepare for action with individuals, families, groups, organizations, and communities

A. Brief Description
This exercise is designed to help you conceptualize what should be the service focus of social workers in the workplace.

B. Objectives
You will:
1. Learn about social work in the workplace.
2. Practice your writing skills.

C. Procedure
1. Social work in the workplace is an emerging field and there is considerable confusion over what should be the major service thrusts. The following list of services might be provided or administered by social workers in the workplace:

   - Day care for children of employees
   - Assistance with financial problems
   - Counseling on family problems
   - Preparation for retirement
   - Programs to combat alienation
   - Assistance with legal problems
   - Assistance in securing health care
   - Counseling on emotional problems
   - Programs to counter alcohol and substance abuse
   - Programs to help people who are laid off by the company
   - Recreation programs
   - Wellness programs
   - Stress management programs
   - Training and staff development programs
   - Advocacy for programs to combat hazardous working conditions

- Consultation on the physical or social environment within the company
- Arranging support groups for employees
- Leading groups established to discuss work-related concerns of workers and management
- Assistance to help strikers meet basic needs
- Fund-raising and planning for community services
- Programs to encourage union membership

2. Write a paper regarding the top five services you believe social workers in the workplace should provide, including a short paragraph stating why you believe each service should be provided.

Competencies/Practice Behaviors Exercise 11.2
Theory X versus Theory Y

Focus Competencies or Practice Behaviors:
- EP 2.1.3a   Distinguish, appraise, and integrate multiple sources of knowledge, including research-based knowledge and practice wisdom
- EP 2.1.3b   Analyze models of assessment, prevention, intervention, and evaluation
- EP 2.1.7a   Utilize conceptual frameworks to guide the processes of assessment, intervention, and evaluation
- EP 2.1.7b   Critique and apply knowledge to understand person and environment
- EP 2.1.9a   Continuously discover, appraise, and attend to changing locales, populations, scientific and technological developments, and emerging societal trends to provide relevant services
- EP 2.1.10a Substantively and affectively prepare for action with individuals, families, groups, organizations, and communities

A. Brief Description
This exercise is designed to help you become more aware of Theory X and Theory Y styles of management and to assist you in developing an effective management style.

B. Objectives
You will:
1. Understand the differences in management style.
2. Practice your writing skills.

C. Procedure
1. Read about both theories of management (which are presented in the chapter in the text).
2. Write a short paper describing examples of employment you have held under these styles of managers and discuss your feelings about working under them.
3. On a separate sheet of paper, answer the following question: Because Theory Y is apparently superior to Theory X in motivating employees to be creative and productive, why is Theory X used by so many managers.

Competencies/Practice Behaviors Exercise 11.3
Role Play—Theory X versus Theory Y

Focus Competencies or Practice Behaviors:
- EP 2.1.1c   Attend to professional roles and boundaries
- EP 2.1.1d   Demonstrate professional demeanor in behavior, appearance, and communication
- EP 2.1.3a   Distinguish, appraise, and integrate multiple sources of knowledge, including research-based knowledge and practice wisdom
- EP 2.1.3b   Analyze models of assessment, prevention, intervention, and evaluation
- EP 2.1.3c   Demonstrate effective oral and written communication in working with individuals, families, groups, organizations, communities, and colleagues
- EP 2.1.7a   Utilize conceptual frameworks to guide the processes of assessment, intervention, and evaluation
- EP 2.1.7b   Critique and apply knowledge to understand person and environment
- EP 2.1.9a   Continuously discover, appraise, and attend to changing locales, populations, scientific and technological developments, and emerging societal trends to provide relevant services
- EP 2.1.10a   Substantively and affectively prepare for action with individuals, families, groups, organizations, and communities

A. Brief Description
This exercise is designed to help you become more aware of Theory X and Theory Y styles of management and to assist you in developing an effective management style.

B. Objectives
You will:
1. Understand the differences in management style.
2. Practice your oral communication skills.

C. Procedure
1. Read about both theories of management (which are presented in the chapter in the text).
2. Form groups of six—three people proposing Theory X as the management style for the organization, and three people arguing that Theory Y is a better alternative.
3. Role play a board meeting in which you present your case for each style.

Chapter 11 Competencies/Practice Behaviors Exercises Assessment:

Name: _____ Date: _____
Supervisor's Name: _____

Focus Competencies/Practice Behaviors:
- EP 2.1.1c   Attend to professional roles and boundaries
- EP 2.1.1d   Demonstrate professional demeanor in behavior, appearance, and communication
- EP 2.1.3a   Distinguish, appraise, and integrate multiple sources of knowledge, including research-based knowledge and practice wisdom
- EP 2.1.3b   Analyze models of assessment, prevention, intervention, and evaluation
- EP 2.1.3c   Demonstrate effective oral and written communication in working with individuals, families, groups, organizations, communities, and colleagues
- EP 2.1.7a   Utilize conceptual frameworks to guide the processes of assessment, intervention, and evaluation
- EP 2.1.7b   Critique and apply knowledge to understand person and environment
- EP 2.1.9a   Continuously discover, appraise, and attend to changing locales, populations, scientific and technological developments, and emerging societal trends to provide relevant services
- EP 2.1.10a   Substantively and affectively prepare for action with individuals, families, groups, organizations, and communities

Instructions:
A.   Evaluate your work or your partner's work in the Focus Competencies/Practice Behaviors by completing the Competencies/Practice Behaviors Assessment form below
B.   What other Competencies/Practice Behaviors did you use to complete these Exercises? Be sure to record them in your assessments

1.	I have attained this competency/practice behavior (in the range of 81 to 100%)
2.	I have largely attained this competency/practice behavior (in the range of 61 to 80%)
3.	I have partially attained this competency/practice behavior (in the range of 41 to 60%)
4.	I have made a little progress in attaining this competency/practice behavior (in the range of 21 to 40%)
5.	I have made almost no progress in attaining this competency/practice behavior (in the range of 0 to 20%)

EPAS 2008 Core Competencies & Core Practice Behaviors	Student Self Assessment						Evaluator Feedback
Student and Evaluator Assessment Scale and Comments	0	1	2	3	4	5	Agree/Disagree/Comments
EP 2.1.1 Identify as a Professional Social Worker and Conduct Oneself Accordingly:							
a. Advocate for client access to the services of social work							
b. Practice personal reflection and self-correction to assure continual professional development							
c. Attend to professional roles and boundaries							
d. Demonstrate professional demeanor in behavior, appearance, and communication							
e. Engage in career-long learning							
f. Use supervision and consultation							

EP 2.1.2 Apply Social Work Ethical Principles to Guide Professional Practice:						
a.	Recognize and manage personal values in a way that allows professional values to guide practice					
b.	Make ethical decisions by applying NASW Code of Ethics and, as applicable, of the IFSW/IASSW Ethics in Social Work, Statement of Principles					
c.	Tolerate ambiguity in resolving ethical conflicts					
d.	Apply strategies of ethical reasoning to arrive at principled decisions					
EP 2.1.3 Apply Critical Thinking to Inform and Communicate Professional Judgments:						
a.	Distinguish, appraise, and integrate multiple sources of knowledge, including research-based knowledge and practice wisdom					
b.	Analyze models of assessment, prevention, intervention, and evaluation					
c.	Demonstrate effective oral and written communication in working with individuals, families, groups, organizations, communities, and colleagues					
EP 2.1.4 Engage Diversity and Difference in Practice:						
a.	Recognize the extent to which a culture's structures and values may oppress, marginalize, alienate, or create or enhance privilege and power					
b.	Gain sufficient self-awareness to eliminate the influence of personal biases and values in working with diverse groups					
c.	Recognize and communicate their understanding of the importance of difference in shaping life experiences					
d.	View themselves as learners and engage those with whom they work as informants					
EP 2.1.5 Advance Human Rights and Social and Economic Justice:						
a.	Understand forms and mechanisms of oppression and discrimination					
b.	Advocate for human rights and social and economic justice					
c.	Engage in practices that advance social and economic justice					
EP 2.1.6 Engage in Research-Informed Practice and Practice-Informed Research:						
a.	Use practice experience to inform scientific inquiry					
b.	Use research evidence to inform practice					
EP 2.1.7 Apply Knowledge of Human Behavior and the Social Environment:						
a.	Utilize conceptual frameworks to guide the processes of assessment, intervention, and evaluation					
b.	Critique and apply knowledge to understand person and environment					
EP 2.1.8 Engage in Policy Practice to Advance Social and Economic Well-Being and to Deliver Effective Social Work Services:						
a.	Analyze, formulate, and advocate for policies that advance social well-being					
b.	Collaborate with colleagues and clients for effective policy action					

EP 2.1.9 Respond to Contexts that Shape Practice:							
a.	Continuously discover, appraise, and attend to changing locales, populations, scientific and technological developments, and emerging societal trends to provide relevant services						
b.	Provide leadership in promoting sustainable changes in service delivery and practice to improve the quality of social services						
EP 2.1.10 Engage, Assess, Intervene, and Evaluate with Individuals, Families, Groups, Organizations and Communities:							
a.	Substantively and affectively prepare for action with individuals, families, groups, organizations, and communities						
b.	Use empathy and other interpersonal skills						
c.	Develop a mutually agreed-on focus of work and desired outcomes						
d.	Collect, organize, and interpret client data						
e.	Assess client strengths and limitations						
f.	Develop mutually agreed-on intervention goals and objectives						
g.	Select appropriate intervention strategies						
h.	Initiate actions to achieve organizational goals						
i.	Implement prevention interventions that enhance client capacities						
j.	Help clients resolve problems						
k.	Negotiate, mediate, and advocate for clients						
l.	Facilitate transitions and endings						
m.	Critically analyze, monitor, and evaluate interventions						

Chapter 12: Racism, Ethnocentrism, and Strategies For Advancing Social and Economic Justice

Competencies/Practice Behaviors Exercise 12.1
Identifying Prejudices and Stereotypes

Focus Competencies or Practice Behaviors:
- EP 2.1.1b   Practice personal reflection and self-correction to assure continual professional development
- EP 2.1.2a   Recognize and manage personal values in a way that allows professional values to guide practice
- EP 2.1.4a   Recognize the extent to which a culture's structures and values may oppress, marginalize, alienate, or create or enhance privilege and power
- EP 2.1.4b   Gain sufficient self-awareness to eliminate the influence of personal biases and values in working with diverse groups
- EP 2.1.4c   Recognize and communicate their understanding of the importance of difference in shaping life experiences
- EP 2.1.4d   View themselves as learners and engage those with whom they work as informants
- EP 2.1.5a   Understand forms and mechanisms of oppression and discrimination
- EP 2.1.7a   Utilize conceptual frameworks to guide the processes of assessment, intervention, and evaluation
- EP 2.1.8a   Analyze, formulate, and advocate for policies that advance social well-being

A. Brief Description
    This exercise is designed to help you identify and examine your racial and ethnic stereotypes and prejudices.

B. Objectives
    You will:
    1. Become more aware of your personal biases.
    2. Learn to separate your personal views from your professional behavior.

C. Procedure
    1. List on a sheet of paper, five of the following racial or ethnic groups: African Americans, Puerto Ricans, Cubans, Chinese, Vietnamese, Native Americans, Mexicans, Italians, Eskimos, Japanese, Arabs, Norwegians.
    2. List a derogatory remark about each of the racial or ethnic groups and then respond with a positive remark about the group that has been disparaged. The response can be a defense of the group, a retort to the specific negative comment, or a general comment about the stereotype that you have used.
    3. After you have completed the previous section of this exercise, write your answers to the following questions.

    > a. What particular kinds of stereotypes and prejudices emerged?
    > b. Were there any negative comments made that were particularly difficult to respond to? Why?
    > c. Where do stereotypes start?
    > d. What was it like to have to attack, and defend, a particular group?
    > e. If you were a member of an ethnic group in which very negative stereotypes were stated, how would you feel?

Competencies/Practice Behaviors Exercise 12.2
Star Track to New Venus

Focus Competencies or Practice Behaviors:
- EP 2.1.1b   Practice personal reflection and self-correction to assure continual professional development
- EP 2.1.2a   Recognize and manage personal values in a way that allows professional values to guide practice
- EP 2.1.4a   Recognize the extent to which a culture's structures and values may oppress, marginalize, alienate, or create or enhance privilege and power
- EP 2.1.4b   Gain sufficient self-awareness to eliminate the influence of personal biases and values in working with diverse groups
- EP 2.1.4c   Recognize and communicate their understanding of the importance of difference in shaping life experiences
- EP 2.1.4d   View themselves as learners and engage those with whom they work as informants
- EP 2.1.5a   Understand forms and mechanisms of oppression and discrimination
- EP 2.1.7a   Utilize conceptual frameworks to guide the processes of assessment, intervention, and evaluation

A. Brief Description
This exercise is designed to help you identify some of your positive and negative stereotypes about various racial and ethnic groups.

B. Objectives
You will:
1. Become more aware of your own stereotypes.
2. Learn to separate your personal stereotypes from your professional behavior.

C. Procedure
1. Read the following:

> You are living in the year 2024. In 2017 the United States discovered a planet in a distant galaxy that appears to have a climate and atmosphere remarkably similar to Earth's. Scientists are virtually certain that this planet, named New Venus, can support human life. In 2021 the United States began building a new spaceship, named *Star Track*, that will be capable of transporting 20 people to New Venus. *Star Track* has recently been completed. In the year 2024 a new comet, Dark Vadim, is discovered and found to be headed on a collision course with Earth. Scientists predict it will strike at the end of that year. A huge explosion, much worse than a nuclear war, is expected, and many scientists are predicting that Earth will disintegrate. The President of the United States has commissioned you to choose the ethnic and racial backgrounds of the 20 people who will soon board *Star Track* to fly to New Venus in order to continue the human race. The President informs you that you may select the racial and ethnic backgrounds from the following list. Everyone may come from one ethnic or

> racial background or from a variety of backgrounds. After you provide your selection, the President will select, consistent with your choices, people in their 20s, including ten men and ten women. All the people selected will be fluent in the English language.

2. Following is a listing of the possible ethnic and racial groups from which you may choose:

Chinese	German	Japanese	Nicaraguan
French	Vietnamese	Polish	Kenyan
Filipino	Hungarian	Irish	Haitian
Portuguese	Egyptian	Italian	Native American
White American	Saudi Arabian	Iranian	Australian
African American	Israeli	Cuban	Puerto Rican
Hawaiian	Pakistani	Russian	Eskimo
Mexican	Nigerian	Colombian	Samoan

3. Write a list of your choices, and state your reasons for your choices, and why you did not choose people from the racial and ethnic backgrounds that you excluded.

Competencies/Practice Behaviors Exercise 12.3
Racial and Ethnic Prejudices

Focus Competencies or Practice Behaviors:
- EP 2.1.1b Practice personal reflection and self-correction to assure continual professional development
- EP 2.1.2a Recognize and manage personal values in a way that allows professional values to guide practice
- EP 2.1.4a Recognize the extent to which a culture's structures and values may oppress, marginalize, alienate, or create or enhance privilege and power
- EP 2.1.4b Gain sufficient self-awareness to eliminate the influence of personal biases and values in working with diverse groups
- EP 2.1.4c Recognize and communicate their understanding of the importance of difference in shaping life experiences
- EP 2.1.4d View themselves as learners and engage those with whom they work as informants
- EP 2.1.5a Understand forms and mechanisms of oppression and discrimination
- EP 2.1.7a Utilize conceptual frameworks to guide the processes of assessment, intervention, and evaluation

A. Brief Description
This exercise is designed to help you identify your racial and ethnic prejudices and to demonstrate that practically everyone has racial and ethnic stereotypes.

B. Objectives
You will:
1. Become more aware of your own prejudices.
2. Learn to separate your own prejudices from your professional behavior.

C. Procedure
1. Read the following:

> **Selecting a Spouse**
>
> Assume that you are single. Place an X by each of the following groups of which you would be hesitant to marry a member. Your responses will remain anonymous to the class.
>
> | | | | | | |
> |---|---|---|---|---|---|
> | ___ | Russian | ___ Polish | ___ | Brazilian |
> | ___ | Cuban | ___ Norwegian | ___ | Hungarian |
> | ___ | French | ___ Samoan | ___ | Vietnamese |
> | ___ | Mexican | ___ Arab | ___ | Pakistani |
> | ___ | African American | ___ Israeli | ___ | Korean |
> | ___ | Native American | ___ Chinese | ___ | Panamanian |
> | ___ | Puerto Rican | ___ Japanese | ___ | Nigerian |
> | ___ | Italian | ___ Filipino | ___ | Portuguese |
> | ___ | German | ___ White American | ___ | Eskimo |

2. After you have finished this part, write the reasons why you would be hesitant to marry a member of each of the racial and ethnic groups you have checked. In writing your reasons, go beyond general reasons (such as "Parents would disapprove" or "I don't like members of such groups") and identify specific reasons why your parents would disapprove or why you dislike members of certain groups.
3. Answer the following questions:
   a. Does this exercise suggest that practically everyone has racial and ethnic stereotypes and prejudices?
   b. How do such stereotypes and prejudices develop in people?
   c. How would you feel if you were a member of a racial or ethnic group that was being disparaged by others?
   d. How can such stereotypes and prejudices be eradicated?
4. The instructor will read to the class some of the derogatory statements that are made.

Competencies/Practice Behaviors Exercise 12.4
Role Play—What It Feels Like to Be Discriminated Against

Focus Competencies or Practice Behaviors:
- EP 2.1.1b Practice personal reflection and self-correction to assure continual professional development
- EP 2.1.2a Recognize and manage personal values in a way that allows professional values to guide practice
- EP 2.1.4a Recognize the extent to which a culture's structures and values may oppress, marginalize, alienate, or create or enhance privilege and power
- EP 2.1.4b Gain sufficient self-awareness to eliminate the influence of personal biases and values in working with diverse groups
- EP 2.1.4c Recognize and communicate their understanding of the importance of difference in shaping life experiences
- EP 2.1.4d View themselves as learners and engage those with whom they work as informants

- EP 2.1.5a Understand forms and mechanisms of oppression and discrimination
- EP 2.1.7a Utilize conceptual frameworks to guide the processes of assessment, intervention, and evaluation

A. Brief Description
    This exercise is designed to give you an awareness of how it feels to be a victim of discrimination.

B. Objectives
    You will:
    1. Think about discrimination.
    2. Experience the effects of discrimination.

C. Procedure
    1. The instructor will be the moderator of this role play. More information is provided for the moderator in Chapter 12 of the Instructor's Manual.
    2. You will be asked a question that is likely to stimulate a lively discussion, such as "Do you think Affirmative Action programs should be eliminated?" or "Do you think the placement of African American children with white parents for adoption should be encouraged or discouraged?"
    3. You will be asked to raise your hand if you have something to contribute.

Chapter 12 Competencies/Practice Behaviors Exercises Assessment:

Name: _____ Date: _____
Supervisor's Name: _____

Focus Competencies/Practice Behaviors:
- EP 2.1.1b   Practice personal reflection and self-correction to assure continual professional development
- EP 2.1.2a   Recognize and manage personal values in a way that allows professional values to guide practice
- EP 2.1.4a   Recognize the extent to which a culture's structures and values may oppress, marginalize, alienate, or create or enhance privilege and power
- EP 2.1.4b   Gain sufficient self-awareness to eliminate the influence of personal biases and values in working with diverse groups
- EP 2.1.4c   Recognize and communicate their understanding of the importance of difference in shaping life experiences
- EP 2.1.4d   View themselves as learners and engage those with whom they work as informants
- EP 2.1.5a   Understand forms and mechanisms of oppression and discrimination
- EP 2.1.7a   Utilize conceptual frameworks to guide the processes of assessment, intervention, and evaluation
- EP 2.1.8a   Analyze, formulate, and advocate for policies that advance social well-being

Instructions:
A.   Evaluate your work or your partner's work in the Focus Competencies/Practice Behaviors by completing the Competencies/Practice Behaviors Assessment form below
B.   What other Competencies/Practice Behaviors did you use to complete these Exercises? Be sure to record them in your assessments

1.	I have attained this competency/practice behavior (in the range of 81 to 100%)
2.	I have largely attained this competency/practice behavior (in the range of 61 to 80%)
3.	I have partially attained this competency/practice behavior (in the range of 41 to 60%)
4.	I have made a little progress in attaining this competency/practice behavior (in the range of 21 to 40%)
5.	I have made almost no progress in attaining this competency/practice behavior (in the range of 0 to 20%)

EPAS 2008 Core Competencies & Core Practice Behaviors	Student Self Assessment						Evaluator Feedback
Student and Evaluator Assessment Scale and Comments	0	1	2	3	4	5	Agree/Disagree/Comments
EP 2.1.1 Identify as a Professional Social Worker and Conduct Oneself Accordingly:							
a. Advocate for client access to the services of social work							
b. Practice personal reflection and self-correction to assure continual professional development							
c. Attend to professional roles and boundaries							
d. Demonstrate professional demeanor in behavior, appearance, and communication							
e. Engage in career-long learning							
f. Use supervision and consultation							

EP 2.1.2 Apply Social Work Ethical Principles to Guide Professional Practice:						
a.	Recognize and manage personal values in a way that allows professional values to guide practice					
b.	Make ethical decisions by applying NASW Code of Ethics and, as applicable, of the IFSW/IASSW Ethics in Social Work, Statement of Principles					
c.	Tolerate ambiguity in resolving ethical conflicts					
d.	Apply strategies of ethical reasoning to arrive at principled decisions					
EP 2.1.3 Apply Critical Thinking to Inform and Communicate Professional Judgments:						
a.	Distinguish, appraise, and integrate multiple sources of knowledge, including research-based knowledge and practice wisdom					
b.	Analyze models of assessment, prevention, intervention, and evaluation					
c.	Demonstrate effective oral and written communication in working with individuals, families, groups, organizations, communities, and colleagues					
EP 2.1.4 Engage Diversity and Difference in Practice:						
a.	Recognize the extent to which a culture's structures and values may oppress, marginalize, alienate, or create or enhance privilege and power					
b.	Gain sufficient self-awareness to eliminate the influence of personal biases and values in working with diverse groups					
c.	Recognize and communicate their understanding of the importance of difference in shaping life experiences					
d.	View themselves as learners and engage those with whom they work as informants					
EP 2.1.5 Advance Human Rights and Social and Economic Justice:						
a.	Understand forms and mechanisms of oppression and discrimination					
b.	Advocate for human rights and social and economic justice					
c.	Engage in practices that advance social and economic justice					
EP 2.1.6 Engage in Research-Informed Practice and Practice-Informed Research:						
a.	Use practice experience to inform scientific inquiry					
b.	Use research evidence to inform practice					
EP 2.1.7 Apply Knowledge of Human Behavior and the Social Environment:						
a.	Utilize conceptual frameworks to guide the processes of assessment, intervention, and evaluation					
b.	Critique and apply knowledge to understand person and environment					
EP 2.1.8 Engage in Policy Practice to Advance Social and Economic Well-Being and to Deliver Effective Social Work Services:						
a.	Analyze, formulate, and advocate for policies that advance social well-being					
b.	Collaborate with colleagues and clients for effective policy action					

	EP 2.1.9 Respond to Contexts that Shape Practice:						
a.	Continuously discover, appraise, and attend to changing locales, populations, scientific and technological developments, and emerging societal trends to provide relevant services						
b.	Provide leadership in promoting sustainable changes in service delivery and practice to improve the quality of social services						
	EP 2.1.10 Engage, Assess, Intervene, and Evaluate with Individuals, Families, Groups, Organizations and Communities:						
a.	Substantively and affectively prepare for action with individuals, families, groups, organizations, and communities						
b.	Use empathy and other interpersonal skills						
c.	Develop a mutually agreed-on focus of work and desired outcomes						
d.	Collect, organize, and interpret client data						
e.	Assess client strengths and limitations						
f.	Develop mutually agreed-on intervention goals and objectives						
g.	Select appropriate intervention strategies						
h.	Initiate actions to achieve organizational goals						
i.	Implement prevention interventions that enhance client capacities						
j.	Help clients resolve problems						
k.	Negotiate, mediate, and advocate for clients						
l.	Facilitate transitions and endings						
m.	Critically analyze, monitor, and evaluate interventions						

Chapter 13: Sexism and Efforts for Achieving Equality

Competencies/Practice Behaviors Exercise 13.1
Male and Female Stereotypes

Focus Competencies or Practice Behaviors:
- EP 2.1.1b   Practice personal reflection and self-correction to assure continual professional development
- EP 2.1.2a   Recognize and manage personal values in a way that allows professional values to guide practice
- EP 2.1.4a   Recognize the extent to which a culture's structures and values may oppress, marginalize, alienate, or create or enhance privilege and power
- EP 2.1.4b   Gain sufficient self-awareness to eliminate the influence of personal biases and values in working with diverse groups
- EP 2.1.4c   Recognize and communicate their understanding of the importance of difference in shaping life experiences
- EP 2.1.4d   View themselves as learners and engage those with whom they work as informants
- EP 2.1.5a   Understand forms and mechanisms of oppression and discrimination
- EP 2.1.7a   Utilize conceptual frameworks to guide the processes of assessment, intervention, and evaluation

A. Brief Description
    This exercise is designed to help you identify and examine some stereotypes about females and males.

B. Objectives
    You will:
    1. Become aware of your own stereotypes.
    2. Learn to separate your personal views from your professional behavior.

C. Procedure
    1. Complete the following questionnaire.

Differences Between Females and Males

1. Males tend to be more competitively oriented than females.
   True   False

2. Females tend to be more concerned about their physical appearance than males.
   True   False

3. It would be a mistake for our country to elect a woman president.
   True   False

4. Females enjoy parenting children more than males.
   True   False

> 5. Males are less emotional than females.
>   True   False
>
> 6. A female should not ask a male out for a date.
>   True   False
>
> 7. Females tend to have more trouble making decisions than males.
>   True   False
>
> 8. Females tend to be smarter than males in academic work.
>   True   False
>
> 9. Males tend to be more mechanically minded than females.
>   True   False
>
> 10. Males should play the dominant role in sexual relationships.
>   True   False
>
> 11. A husband should have a greater responsibility than a wife in meeting the financial needs of a family.
>   True   False
>
> 12. A wife should have a greater responsibility than a husband in raising the children and doing the domestic tasks.
>   True   False

2. On a separate sheet of paper, cite your reason for each of the answers.
3. Volunteers will be asked to record their answers on the blackboard.

Competencies/Practice Behaviors Exercise 13.2
Double Standards

Focus Competencies or Practice Behaviors:
- EP 2.1.1b   Practice personal reflection and self-correction to assure continual professional development
- EP 2.1.2a   Recognize and manage personal values in a way that allows professional values to guide practice
- EP 2.1.4a   Recognize the extent to which a culture's structures and values may oppress, marginalize, alienate, or create or enhance privilege and power
- EP 2.1.4b   Gain sufficient self-awareness to eliminate the influence of personal biases and values in working with diverse groups
- EP 2.1.4c   Recognize and communicate their understanding of the importance of difference in shaping life experiences
- EP 2.1.4d   View themselves as learners and engage those with whom they work as informants
- EP 2.1.5a   Understand forms and mechanisms of oppression and discrimination
- EP 2.1.7a   Utilize conceptual frameworks to guide the processes of assessment, intervention, and evaluation

A. Brief Description
This exercise is designed to help you identify and examine double standards for male and female interactions.

B. Objectives
You will:
1. Become more aware of your personal views.
2. Be able to separate your personal views from your professional behavior.

C. Procedure
1. Identify double standards in dating relationships, marital relationships, and sexual behaviors between males and females. For example, society generally allows males to be more aggressive and to use more vulgar language; and males are expected to ask females for dates, but females traditionally have been raised to believe they should not ask males for dates. For each double standard that you identify, cite whether you believe the double standard is desirable or undesirable.
2. The double standards, and the desirability of these double standards, will be discussed with the class.

Competencies/Practice Behaviors Exercise 13.3
Learning to Be Assertive

Focus Competencies or Practice Behaviors:
- EP 2.1.1b   Practice personal reflection and self-correction to assure continual professional development
- EP 2.1.3a   Distinguish, appraise, and integrate multiple sources of knowledge, including research-based knowledge and practice wisdom
- EP 2.1.4a   Recognize the extent to which a culture's structures and values may oppress, marginalize, alienate, or create or enhance privilege and power
- EP 2.1.4b   Gain sufficient self-awareness to eliminate the influence of personal biases and values in working with diverse groups
- EP 2.1.5a   Understand forms and mechanisms of oppression and discrimination
- EP 2.1.9a   Continuously discover, appraise, and attend to changing locales, populations, scientific and technological developments, and emerging societal trends to provide relevant services

A. Brief Description
This exercise is designed to help you learn how to be assertive in problematic interactions where in the past you were either nonassertive or aggressive.

B. Objectives
You will:
1. Learn the differences between assertive, nonassertive, and aggressive behavior.
2. Understand assertiveness training, and why it is important for social work.

C. Procedure
1. Identify a situation in the past in which you wished you had been assertive, rather than aggressive or nonassertive. Some examples follow: The situation may involve being told to do something you did not want to do. Or, perhaps someone was smoking a cigarette near you, which bothered you. Or, perhaps someone made a put-down comment about

you. Or, perhaps you're unable to express what you feel about certain situations to your parents, or to someone you're dating.
2. The instructor will state the following:

> We will now do a visualization exercise that is designed to help you learn to be more assertive in the situation you identified. There will be no tricks in this exercise. Close your eyes and keep them closed during this exercise. Get as comfortable as possible in your chair, and slowly take a couple of deep breaths to become relaxed.
>
> Focus on a specific incident in your past when you wanted to be assertive, but instead were either nonassertive or aggressive. Visualize all the details of what happened. *(Pause a few seconds after asking each of the following questions.)* What was said to you? What did you fail to say that you wanted to say? What did you say that you didn't want to say? How did you feel about what was said? How do you now feel about this incident? Your nonverbal communication is as important in being assertive as is verbal communication. Think about your nonverbal communication. What did you communicate with your facial expressions? What did you communicate with your body posture? Did you look down or away from the other person? Did you glare at the other person? What did your gestures communicate? What was your voice tone and volume like? Did your voice crack? Did you yell or speak softly? Did you speak rapidly or with hesitation? During this incident which of your verbal and nonverbal communications were nonassertive? Which were aggressive? Which were assertive?
>
> Now, let's turn to focus on how to handle this situation more assertively when it arises again. Continue to keep your eyes closed. What might you say that would assertively handle this situation? *(Pause.)* What changes do you need to make in your nonverbal communication to present yourself more assertively? *(Pause.)* Is there someone you know who would be good at handling this situation assertively? *(Pause.)* If there is someone, what would this person say or do? *(Pause.)* Does this assertive mode give you some ideas on how you might assertively handle this situation? *(Pause.)*
>
> Continue to visualize various approaches that might work for you. Also, visualize yourself using each of these approaches. For each approach, imagine the full set of interactions that would occur if you were to use the approach. *(Pause.)*
>
> Now, seek to select an assertive approach that you believe would best work for you when the nonassertive or aggressive situation arises again in the future. Are you now sufficiently prepared and confident to use this approach in a real-life situation? If not, you may want to visualize further what you might say or do to increase your confidence. Or, you may want to select another approach that you would be more comfortable in using. Or, you may want to role-play your approach with a friend so that you become more comfortable in using the approach. *(Pause.)*
>
> The real test will come when you try out your assertive approach in a real-life situation. The next time your problematic situation arises, seek to use your assertive approach. After trying it out, analyze how it turned out. Pat yourself on the back for what you did well. Identify aspects of your nonverbal and verbal communication that you need to improve in order to express yourself more assertively. Visualize ways in which you might more assertively express yourself in the areas you need to work on.

> Above all, congratulate yourself on your efforts to become more assertive. You've earned feeling good about yourself. Learning to express yourself in situations that you're comfortable in is one of the greatest thrills you'll ever experience. OK, gradually open your eyes, and take a little while to relax.

3. You will be asked whether you have any questions or comments about the exercise. Then asked if there are any situations you would like to see others in the class role-play.

Competencies/Practice Behaviors Exercise 13.4
Sexist Words

Focus Competencies or Practice Behaviors:
- EP 2.1.1b Practice personal reflection and self-correction to assure continual professional development
- EP 2.1.3a Distinguish, appraise, and integrate multiple sources of knowledge, including research-based knowledge and practice wisdom
- EP 2.1.4a Recognize the extent to which a culture's structures and values may oppress, marginalize, alienate, or create or enhance privilege and power
- EP 2.1.4b Gain sufficient self-awareness to eliminate the influence of personal biases and values in working with diverse groups
- EP 2.1.5a Understand forms and mechanisms of oppression and discrimination

A. Brief Description
This exercise is designed to help you explore the pervasiveness of sexist words in our society.

B. Objectives
You will:
1. Become more aware of the pervasiveness of sexist words in our society.
2. Learn to avoid using these words.

C. Procedure
1. The words we select to use greatly affect our interpretation of reality. The use of sexist words in our society has been a significant factor in defining and maintaining the position of dominant males, with females being assigned a supportive or submissive role. Many English words reflect an aura of sexism. For instance, the following words and phrases are considered to be sexist:

mankind	man and wife
chairman	he (when referring to someone who may be a
salesman	male or female)
congressman	man of God
policeman	man-made
man-to-man	best man for the job

Yet there are a number of other words that have *man*, *men*, or *male* as a component. These words include:

female	manner	menstruate
human	mantle	menstruation
manage	mantra	mental

management	manual	mentality
manager	manufacture	mention
mandate	menarche	mentor
mandatory	menopause	menu
man hole	menorrhagia	woman
manicure	mense	women
manifest	menses	
manifold	menstrual	

2. Write a report stating which words appear to be sexist. Also discuss why words that relate primarily to biological functioning among women (such as menses, menstruation, and menopause) have "men" as a component. Volunteers will be asked to share their opinions and conclusions with the whole class.

Competencies/Practice Behaviors Exercise 13.5
Role Play—Male and Female Stereotypes

Focus Competencies or Practice Behaviors:
- EP 2.1.1b Practice personal reflection and self-correction to assure continual professional development
- EP 2.1.2a Recognize and manage personal values in a way that allows professional values to guide practice
- EP 2.1.4a Recognize the extent to which a culture's structures and values may oppress, marginalize, alienate, or create or enhance privilege and power
- EP 2.1.4b Gain sufficient self-awareness to eliminate the influence of personal biases and values in working with diverse groups
- EP 2.1.4c Recognize and communicate their understanding of the importance of difference in shaping life experiences
- EP 2.1.4d View themselves as learners and engage those with whom they work as informants
- EP 2.1.5a Understand forms and mechanisms of oppression and discrimination
- EP 2.1.7a Utilize conceptual frameworks to guide the processes of assessment, intervention, and evaluation

A. Brief Description
This role play is designed to help you identify and examine some stereotypes about females and males.

B. Objectives
You will:
1. Become aware of your own stereotypes.
2. Learn to separate your personal views from your professional behavior.

C. Procedure
1. Separate into two groups. One group will begin the role play by arguing that all the following statements are true, including the reasons for this argument. The other group will debate that all the following statements are false, again, citing reasons why.

Differences Between Females and Males

1. Males tend to be more competitively oriented than females.
   True   False

2. Females tend to be more concerned about their physical appearance than males.
   True   False

3. It would be a mistake for our country to elect a woman president.
   True   False

4. Females enjoy parenting children more than males.
   True   False

5. Males are less emotional than females.
   True   False

6. A female should not ask a male out for a date.
   True   False

7. Females tend to have more trouble making decisions than males.
   True   False

8. Females tend to be smarter than males in academic work.
   True   False

9. Males tend to be more mechanically minded than females.
   True   False

10. Males should play the dominant role in sexual relationships.
    True   False

11. A husband should have a greater responsibility than a wife in meeting the financial needs of a family.
    True   False

12. A wife should have a greater responsibility than a husband in raising the children and doing the domestic tasks.
    True   False

2. Begin a discussion after the role play about the difficulties of debating for or against something that is in direct opposition of your own personal views.

Chapter 13 Competencies/Practice Behaviors Exercises Assessment:

Name: _____ Date: _____
Supervisor's Name: _____

Focus Competencies/Practice Behaviors:
- EP 2.1.1b   Practice personal reflection and self-correction to assure continual professional development
- EP 2.1.2a   Recognize and manage personal values in a way that allows professional values to guide practice
- EP 2.1.3a   Distinguish, appraise, and integrate multiple sources of knowledge, including research-based knowledge and practice wisdom
- EP 2.1.4a   Recognize the extent to which a culture's structures and values may oppress, marginalize, alienate, or create or enhance privilege and power
- EP 2.1.4b   Gain sufficient self-awareness to eliminate the influence of personal biases and values in working with diverse groups
- EP 2.1.4c   Recognize and communicate their understanding of the importance of difference in shaping life experiences
- EP 2.1.4d   View themselves as learners and engage those with whom they work as informants
- EP 2.1.5a   Understand forms and mechanisms of oppression and discrimination
- EP 2.1.7a   Utilize conceptual frameworks to guide the processes of assessment, intervention, and evaluation
- EP 2.1.9a   Continuously discover, appraise, and attend to changing locales, populations, scientific and technological developments, and emerging societal trends to provide relevant services

Instructions:
A.   Evaluate your work or your partner's work in the Focus Competencies/Practice Behaviors by completing the Competencies/Practice Behaviors Assessment form below
B.   What other Competencies/Practice Behaviors did you use to complete these Exercises? Be sure to record them in your assessments

1.	I have attained this competency/practice behavior (in the range of 81 to 100%)
2.	I have largely attained this competency/practice behavior (in the range of 61 to 80%)
3.	I have partially attained this competency/practice behavior (in the range of 41 to 60%)
4.	I have made a little progress in attaining this competency/practice behavior (in the range of 21 to 40%)
5.	I have made almost no progress in attaining this competency/practice behavior (in the range of 0 to 20%)

EPAS 2008 Core Competencies & Core Practice Behaviors	Student Self Assessment						Evaluator Feedback
Student and Evaluator Assessment Scale and Comments	0	1	2	3	4	5	Agree/Disagree/Comments
EP 2.1.1 Identify as a Professional Social Worker and Conduct Oneself Accordingly:							
a. Advocate for client access to the services of social work							
b. Practice personal reflection and self-correction to assure continual professional development							
c. Attend to professional roles and boundaries							
d. Demonstrate professional demeanor in behavior, appearance, and communication							
e. Engage in career-long learning							
f. Use supervision and consultation							

EP 2.1.2 Apply Social Work Ethical Principles to Guide Professional Practice:						
a. Recognize and manage personal values in a way that allows professional values to guide practice						
b. Make ethical decisions by applying NASW Code of Ethics and, as applicable, of the IFSW/IASSW Ethics in Social Work, Statement of Principles						
c. Tolerate ambiguity in resolving ethical conflicts						
d. Apply strategies of ethical reasoning to arrive at principled decisions						
EP 2.1.3 Apply Critical Thinking to Inform and Communicate Professional Judgments:						
a. Distinguish, appraise, and integrate multiple sources of knowledge, including research-based knowledge and practice wisdom						
b. Analyze models of assessment, prevention, intervention, and evaluation						
c. Demonstrate effective oral and written communication in working with individuals, families, groups, organizations, communities, and colleagues						
EP 2.1.4 Engage Diversity and Difference in Practice:						
a. Recognize the extent to which a culture's structures and values may oppress, marginalize, alienate, or create or enhance privilege and power						
b. Gain sufficient self-awareness to eliminate the influence of personal biases and values in working with diverse groups						
c. Recognize and communicate their understanding of the importance of difference in shaping life experiences						
d. View themselves as learners and engage those with whom they work as informants						
EP 2.1.5 Advance Human Rights and Social and Economic Justice:						
a. Understand forms and mechanisms of oppression and discrimination						
b. Advocate for human rights and social and economic justice						
c. Engage in practices that advance social and economic justice						
EP 2.1.6 Engage in Research-Informed Practice and Practice-Informed Research:						
a. Use practice experience to inform scientific inquiry						
b. Use research evidence to inform practice						
EP 2.1.7 Apply Knowledge of Human Behavior and the Social Environment:						
a. Utilize conceptual frameworks to guide the processes of assessment, intervention, and evaluation						
b. Critique and apply knowledge to understand person and environment						
EP 2.1.8 Engage in Policy Practice to Advance Social and Economic Well-Being and to Deliver Effective Social Work Services:						
a. Analyze, formulate, and advocate for policies that advance social well-being						
b. Collaborate with colleagues and clients for effective policy action						

EP 2.1.9 Respond to Contexts that Shape Practice:						
a. Continuously discover, appraise, and attend to changing locales, populations, scientific and technological developments, and emerging societal trends to provide relevant services						
b. Provide leadership in promoting sustainable changes in service delivery and practice to improve the quality of social services						
EP 2.1.10 Engage, Assess, Intervene, and Evaluate with Individuals, Families, Groups, Organizations and Communities:						
a. Substantively and affectively prepare for action with individuals, families, groups, organizations, and communities						
b. Use empathy and other interpersonal skills						
c. Develop a mutually agreed-on focus of work and desired outcomes						
d. Collect, organize, and interpret client data						
e. Assess client strengths and limitations						
f. Develop mutually agreed-on intervention goals and objectives						
g. Select appropriate intervention strategies						
h. Initiate actions to achieve organizational goals						
i. Implement prevention interventions that enhance client capacities						
j. Help clients resolve problems						
k. Negotiate, mediate, and advocate for clients						
l. Facilitate transitions and endings						
m. Critically analyze, monitor, and evaluate interventions						

Chapter 14: Aging and Gerontological Services

Competencies/Practice Behaviors Exercise 14.1
Values Clarification About Later Adulthood

Focus Competencies or Practice Behaviors:
- EP 2.1.1b   Practice personal reflection and self-correction to assure continual professional development
- EP 2.1.1e   Engage in career-long learning
- EP 2.1.4a   Recognize the extent to which a culture's structures and values may oppress, marginalize, alienate, or create or enhance privilege and power
- EP 2.1.4b   Gain sufficient self-awareness to eliminate the influence of personal biases and values in working with diverse groups
- EP 2.1.8a   Analyze, formulate, and advocate for policies that advance social well-being

A. Brief Description
   This exercise is designed to have you become more aware of your attitudes and values regarding later adulthood.

B. Objectives
   You will:
   1. Discover your beliefs about later adulthood.

C. Procedure
   1. Complete the following questionnaire. Individual responses will remain anonymous to the class.

Values Regarding Later Adulthood

1. Do you believe that most people over the age of 65 are physically attractive?
   a. Yes
   b. No
   c. Uncertain

2. Do you believe that it is desirable for older adults to be sexually active?
   a. Yes
   b. No
   c. Uncertain

3. Do you want to spend the last few years of your life in a nursing home?
   a. Yes
   b. No
   c. Uncertain

4. If one of your parents dies, would you want the other to remarry?
   a. Yes
   b. No
   c. Uncertain

5. If an older adult has a terminal illness, is in severe pain, and has no hope of recovery, do you think that this person has the right to terminate his or her life by suicide?
   a. Yes
   b. No
   c. Uncertain

6. Do you believe that older adults should be forced to retire when they reach a certain age, such as age 70?
   a. Yes
   b. No
   c. Uncertain

7. If an older adult has a terminal illness and is in a coma, do you believe that person should be kept alive by life-sustaining equipment?
   a. Yes
   b. No
   c. Uncertain

8. How old would you like to be when you die?
   _____ years of age

9. If you were 70 years of age, which would you prefer?
   a. Continue to work to maintain your standard of living
   b. Retire, which would bring about a sharp reduction in your standard of living
   c. Uncertain

10. If you were 75 years of age and had heart disease that was terminal, which would you prefer?
    a. A heart transplant in an attempt to live longer
    b. The less painful choice of saying "no" to a heart transplant and letting nature take its course
    c. Uncertain

11. If you were 80 years of age and your physical capacities had deteriorated substantially, which would you prefer?
    a. Be placed in a nursing home
    b. Continue living in your own home, where you are unlikely to meet your basic needs and therefore may die
    c. Uncertain

> 12. If you were 75 years of age, which of the following choices would you prefer?
>   a. Die fairly suddenly with your physical and mental capacities still intact
>   b. Continue living for 20 more years, but with your physical and mental capacities so deteriorated that you must spend these last 20 years in a nursing home
>   c. Uncertain
>
> 13. If you lived in a nursing home from the age of 80 until you were 100, do you think it would be fair to younger taxpayers to have to pay your expenses through the Social Security system?
>   a. Yes
>   b. No
>   c. Uncertain
>
> 14. Assume that one of your parents has died. If the remaining parent becomes fairly disabled physically (but is still mentally alert), would you allow that parent to live alone in his or her home if he or she desires this alternative, even though life-threatening conditions are likely to arise?
>   a. Yes
>   b. No
>   c. Uncertain
>
> 15. Assume that you are married and have young children. If your only surviving parent becomes fairly disabled (both mentally and physically), which of the following alternatives would you choose?
>   a. Allow the parent to live with you, disrupting your family and forcing family members to provide 24-hour care each day
>   b. Place the parent in a nursing home
>   c. Uncertain
>
> 16. Do you think that middle-aged adults have an obligation to physically take care of their parents comparable to the obligation that parents have to take care of their children?
>   a. Yes, they have a comparable obligation
>   b. No, they do not have a comparable obligation
>   c. Uncertain

2. Review your answers and write a short report regarding whether any of your answers surprised you, and how you feel about your answers.
3. Each question will be discussed in class, and volunteers will be asked to share their responses.

Competencies/Practice Behaviors Exercise 14.2
Saving the Social Security System from Bankruptcy

Focus Competencies or Practice Behaviors:
- EP 2.1.1b Practice personal reflection and self-correction to assure continual professional development
- EP 2.1.3a Distinguish, appraise, and integrate multiple sources of knowledge, including research-based knowledge and practice wisdom
- EP 2.1.4a Recognize the extent to which a culture's structures and values may oppress, marginalize, alienate, or create or enhance privilege and power
- EP 2.1.6b Use research evidence to inform practice
- EP 2.1.7a Utilize conceptual frameworks to guide the processes of assessment, intervention, and evaluation
- EP 2.1.7b Critique and apply knowledge to understand person and environment
- EP 2.1.8a Analyze, formulate, and advocate for policies that advance social well-being

A. Brief Description

You will be able to (a) understand the serious financial plight of the Social Security system, (b) explain to others why the Social Security system in future years may not be able to financially maintain the elderly, and (c) state alternatives for saving the Social Security system from bankruptcy and evaluate the pros and cons of each.

B. Objectives
You will:
1. Gain insight into the problems of the Social Security system.
2. Be more aware of the alternatives being discussed regarding the Social Security system.

C. Procedure
1. The chapter indicates that (a) the Social Security system is in financial trouble; (b) there will in future years be more recipients as people live longer; (c) monthly benefit payments are already inadequate to financially maintain the elderly; and (d) Social Security taxes have increased dramatically, with the maximum tax on an employee increasing from about $400 in 1971 to over $5000 at the present time.
2. Read and then rank from 1 to 6 the following alternatives for trying to save the Social Security system from bankruptcy, with rank number 1 being the most preferred alternative. List the merits and shortcomings of each alternative.

Alternatives
a. Continue to raise the maximum tax on Social Security an average of $250 per year. This amount is approximately the current average increase.
b. Withhold highly expensive medical care from those over age 75. For example, those over 75 would not receive kidney dialysis. Less expensive medical care would continue to be provided.
c. For those over 85, do not provide any medical treatment for life-threatening illnesses, such as cancer, heart attacks, or pneumonia. Treatment for minor ailments, such as colds and arthritis, would continue to be given.

> d. Use euthanasia for those in a nursing home who meet both of the following conditions: (a) have no chance of returning to society, and (b) sincerely express (for at least a two-month period) a wish to die.
>
> e. Encourage older adults to continue to work as long as they are productive. With this approach, working older adults would be paying into the Social Security system.
>
> f. Sharply reduce the benefits paid out of the Social Security system. With this approach, many of the current recipients would be deeply impoverished.

Competencies/Practice Behaviors Exercise 14.3
Interviewing an Older Adult

Focus Competencies or Practice Behaviors:
- EP 2.1.1b   Practice personal reflection and self-correction to assure continual professional development
- EP 2.1.3a   Distinguish, appraise, and integrate multiple sources of knowledge, including research-based knowledge and practice wisdom
- EP 2.1.4a   Recognize the extent to which a culture's structures and values may oppress, marginalize, alienate, or create or enhance privilege and power
- EP 2.1.7a   Utilize conceptual frameworks to guide the processes of assessment, intervention, and evaluation
- EP 2.1.10a   Substantively and affectively prepare for action with individuals, families, groups, organizations, and communities

A. Brief Description
You will gain an appreciation of what it is like to be an older adult in our society, and will be motivated to have more contact and communication with the older adults who are relatives, friends, and acquaintances in your lives.

B. Objectives
You will:
1. Practice your interviewing skills.
2. Learn more about the life experiences of older adults.

C. Procedure
1. Interview an older adult who is still active and who has had interesting life experiences.
2. Possible questions are:
    a. Ask age and when and where born.
    b. Ask what she did for a living (can include housewife and mother).
    c. Ask how old she "feels"—younger than age, older, etc.
    d. Talk about what her plans are for the coming months and years—what would she like to do, accomplish?
    e. Would she still like to learn something entirely new—a new job, hobby, or something she always wanted to learn about?

f. In looking back on life, what are some things she feels like she's learned that younger people should know about? (Give a few minutes or seconds to think here).
g. Are there things she'd like to go back and do over again?
h. About friends and family—what has she learned about relationships that are important?
i. What are her views as to the major social problems confronting older adults in our society?
j. Ask what are her most memorable high points, and low points in life.
k. Does she think she "grew up" in the manner that her parents hoped? That is, does she think her own parents would be satisfied with how she turned out? Why or why not?
l. If she could advise you about "life," what is the most important thing she could say to you at your age?
3. When the interview ends, remember to thank the interviewee.
4. Write a report listing the questions you asked, and the answers you received from your interviewee. Include your own thoughts about the answers, and anything you learned from this exercise.

Competencies/Practice Behaviors Exercise 14.4
Role Play—Physician Assisted Suicide

Focus Competencies or Practice Behaviors:
- EP 2.1.1b Practice personal reflection and self-correction to assure continual professional development
- EP 2.1.2a Recognize and manage personal values in a way that allows professional values to guide practice
- EP 2.1.3a Distinguish, appraise, and integrate multiple sources of knowledge, including research-based knowledge and practice wisdom
- EP 2.1.3c Demonstrate effective oral and written communication in working with individuals, families, groups, organizations, communities, and colleagues
- EP 2.1.4c Recognize and communicate their understanding of the importance of difference in shaping life experiences
- EP 2.1.7a Utilize conceptual frameworks to guide the processes of assessment, intervention, and evaluation
- EP 2.1.7b Critique and apply knowledge to understand person and environment

A. Brief Description
You will better understand the arguments on both sides of the physical-assisted suicide issue, and will clarify your values on this national issue.

B. Objectives
You will:
1. Experience the heart-wrenching decisions regarding terminal illness.
2. Become more familiar with the issue of legalizing physician-assisted suicide.

C. Procedure
1. Read and think about the following scenario:

> Gizelle is a 75-year-old grandmother who has terminal throat cancer. She has had her voice box removed and can only communicate in writing. She has been bedridden for a year and needs constant care. She has to be fed through a feeding tube in her stomach and receives her medicine through a tube in her throat.
>
> Her husband, Oscar, has been trying to meet her needs by himself and is totally exhausted. He has refused hospice care and wants to care for Gizelle by himself, although the grandchildren believe that he has been making mistakes with her medicine.
>
> Physician-assisted suicide has been legalized in their state, but he is adamantly against it, and believes that it is a mortal sin. Gizelle begs him and her grandchildren to have this performed because she can't stand the pain any longer.
>
> Gizelle and Oscar's granddaughter, Crystal, agrees with her grandmother and doesn't want her to suffer any longer. Crystal's brother, Conrad, is against physician-assisted suicide.

2. Begin the role play by forming groups of five. Each playing a member of the family and one portraying the physician who is there to assist in the suicide, should it be permitted, and to answer any questions the family members might ask.
3. After 15 to 20 minutes, each of the groups will come back to the class and discuss the difficulties of trying to make life-and-death decisions.

Chapter 14 Competencies/Practice Behaviors Exercises Assessment:

Name: _____ **Date:** _____
Supervisor's Name: _____

Focus Competencies/Practice Behaviors:
- EP 2.1.1b   Practice personal reflection and self-correction to assure continual professional development
- EP 2.1.1e   Engage in career-long learning
- EP 2.1.2a   Recognize and manage personal values in a way that allows professional values to guide practice
- EP 2.1.3a   Distinguish, appraise, and integrate multiple sources of knowledge, including research-based knowledge and practice wisdom
- EP 2.1.4a   Recognize the extent to which a culture's structures and values may oppress, marginalize, alienate, or create or enhance privilege and power
- EP 2.1.4b   Gain sufficient self-awareness to eliminate the influence of personal biases and values in working with diverse groups
- EP 2.1.6b   Use research evidence to inform practice
- EP 2.1.7a   Utilize conceptual frameworks to guide the processes of assessment, intervention, and evaluation
- EP 2.1.7b   Critique and apply knowledge to understand person and environment
- EP 2.1.8a   Analyze, formulate, and advocate for policies that advance social well-being
- EP 2.1.10a Substantively and affectively prepare for action with individuals, families, groups, organizations, and communities

Instructions:
A.   Evaluate your work or your partner's work in the Focus Competencies/Practice Behaviors by completing the Competencies/Practice Behaviors Assessment form below
B.   What other Competencies/Practice Behaviors did you use to complete these Exercises? Be sure to record them in your assessments

1.	I have attained this competency/practice behavior (in the range of 81 to 100%)
2.	I have largely attained this competency/practice behavior (in the range of 61 to 80%)
3.	I have partially attained this competency/practice behavior (in the range of 41 to 60%)
4.	I have made a little progress in attaining this competency/practice behavior (in the range of 21 to 40%)
5.	I have made almost no progress in attaining this competency/practice behavior (in the range of 0 to 20%)

EPAS 2008 Core Competencies & Core Practice Behaviors	Student Self Assessment						Evaluator Feedback
Student and Evaluator Assessment Scale and Comments	0	1	2	3	4	5	Agree/Disagree/Comments
EP 2.1.1 Identify as a Professional Social Worker and Conduct Oneself Accordingly:							
a. Advocate for client access to the services of social work							
b. Practice personal reflection and self-correction to assure continual professional development							
c. Attend to professional roles and boundaries							
d. Demonstrate professional demeanor in behavior, appearance, and communication							
e. Engage in career-long learning							
f. Use supervision and consultation							

EP 2.1.2 Apply Social Work Ethical Principles to Guide Professional Practice:						
a.	Recognize and manage personal values in a way that allows professional values to guide practice					
b.	Make ethical decisions by applying NASW Code of Ethics and, as applicable, of the IFSW/IASSW Ethics in Social Work, Statement of Principles					
c.	Tolerate ambiguity in resolving ethical conflicts					
d.	Apply strategies of ethical reasoning to arrive at principled decisions					
EP 2.1.3 Apply Critical Thinking to Inform and Communicate Professional Judgments:						
a.	Distinguish, appraise, and integrate multiple sources of knowledge, including research-based knowledge and practice wisdom					
b.	Analyze models of assessment, prevention, intervention, and evaluation					
c.	Demonstrate effective oral and written communication in working with individuals, families, groups, organizations, communities, and colleagues					
EP 2.1.4 Engage Diversity and Difference in Practice:						
a.	Recognize the extent to which a culture's structures and values may oppress, marginalize, alienate, or create or enhance privilege and power					
b.	Gain sufficient self-awareness to eliminate the influence of personal biases and values in working with diverse groups					
c.	Recognize and communicate their understanding of the importance of difference in shaping life experiences					
d.	View themselves as learners and engage those with whom they work as informants					
EP 2.1.5 Advance Human Rights and Social and Economic Justice:						
a.	Understand forms and mechanisms of oppression and discrimination					
b.	Advocate for human rights and social and economic justice					
c.	Engage in practices that advance social and economic justice					
EP 2.1.6 Engage in Research-Informed Practice and Practice-Informed Research:						
a.	Use practice experience to inform scientific inquiry					
b.	Use research evidence to inform practice					
EP 2.1.7 Apply Knowledge of Human Behavior and the Social Environment:						
a.	Utilize conceptual frameworks to guide the processes of assessment, intervention, and evaluation					
b.	Critique and apply knowledge to understand person and environment					
EP 2.1.8 Engage in Policy Practice to Advance Social and Economic Well-Being and to Deliver Effective Social Work Services:						
a.	Analyze, formulate, and advocate for policies that advance social well-being					
b.	Collaborate with colleagues and clients for effective policy action					

	EP 2.1.9 Respond to Contexts that Shape Practice:						
a.	Continuously discover, appraise, and attend to changing locales, populations, scientific and technological developments, and emerging societal trends to provide relevant services						
b.	Provide leadership in promoting sustainable changes in service delivery and practice to improve the quality of social services						
	EP 2.1.10 Engage, Assess, Intervene, and Evaluate with Individuals, Families, Groups, Organizations and Communities:						
a.	Substantively and affectively prepare for action with individuals, families, groups, organizations, and communities						
b.	Use empathy and other interpersonal skills						
c.	Develop a mutually agreed-on focus of work and desired outcomes						
d.	Collect, organize, and interpret client data						
e.	Assess client strengths and limitations						
f.	Develop mutually agreed-on intervention goals and objectives						
g.	Select appropriate intervention strategies						
h.	Initiate actions to achieve organizational goals						
i.	Implement prevention interventions that enhance client capacities						
j.	Help clients resolve problems						
k.	Negotiate, mediate, and advocate for clients						
l.	Facilitate transitions and endings						
m.	Critically analyze, monitor, and evaluate interventions						

Chapter 15: Health Problems and Medical Social Services

Competencies/Practice Behaviors Exercise 15.1
AIDS

Focus Competencies or Practice Behaviors:
- EP 2.1.1b   Practice personal reflection and self-correction to assure continual professional development
- EP 2.1.2a   Recognize and manage personal values in a way that allows professional values to guide practice
- EP 2.1.4b   Gain sufficient self-awareness to eliminate the influence of personal biases and values in working with diverse groups
- EP 2.1.5a   Understand forms and mechanisms of oppression and discrimination
- EP 2.1.7a   Utilize conceptual frameworks to guide the processes of assessment, intervention, and evaluation
- EP 2.1.7b   Critique and apply knowledge to understand person and environment

A.   Brief Description
   This exercise is designed to answer your questions about AIDS.

B.   Objectives
   You will:
   1.   Learn more about AIDS.

C.   Procedure
   1.   Write questions you have about AIDS. Do NOT put your name on the sheets so that anonymity may be retained.
   2.   Prior to the next class period, the instructor will find answers to these questions from knowledgeable authorities or from reliable written information. (If possible, the instructor will invite an authority to answer these questions at the next class period.)

Competencies/Practice Behaviors Exercise 15.2
Handling Medical Social Work Cases

Focus Competencies or Practice Behaviors:
- EP 2.1.1b   Practice personal reflection and self-correction to assure continual professional development
- EP 2.1.2a   Recognize and manage personal values in a way that allows professional values to guide practice
- EP 2.1.2b   Make ethical decisions by applying standards of the National Association of Social Workers Code of Ethics and, as applicable, of the International Federation of Social Workers/International Association of Schools of Social Work Ethics in Social Work, Statement of Principles
- EP 2.1.2d   Apply strategies of ethical reasoning to arrive at principled decisions

- EP 2.1.7a Utilize conceptual frameworks to guide the processes of assessment, intervention, and evaluation
- EP 2.1.10a Substantively and affectively prepare for action with individuals, families, groups, organizations, and communities

A. Brief Description
This exercise is designed to give you simulated experience in medical social work cases and to help you examine some value issues in health care.

B. Objectives
You will:
1. Better understand medical social work.
2. Be able to begin to separate your personal values from your professional behavior.

C. Procedure
1. Write a paper discussing how you would handle each case.

> **Case Example 1:**
> Dr. Stern requests that you (a medical social worker) talk to Frank Kale, who has a type of cancer that is almost always fatal. Dr. Stern wants you to obtain Mr. Kale's written permission for surgery to remove malignant tumors. You meet with Mr. Kale, and he informs you that he already has had four similar painful operations, is now resigned to his life ending, and in no way wants additional surgery. He further states that he wants to return home and live his final days there. He appears rational. You then meet with his wife, who supports her husband's wishes. You inform Dr. Stern of what the Kales have said, and he tells you angrily that he knows what is best for his patients and again instructs you to obtain Mr. Kale's signature. What would you do?

> **Case Example 2:**
> Linda Lightner, a 19-year-old single woman, is admitted late at night to the hospital after being raped and assaulted by a 39-year-old married man. Ms. Lightner, who stated that she used to baby-sit for the perpetrator's family, is given medical treatment. You're a social worker at this hospital, and you meet with the victim the next day. She is scared, deeply hurt emotionally, very angry, and occasionally tearful. She is afraid to tell her partner, whom she'll be seeing in two days, for fear that he'll break off their relationship. She also states that she has heard rumors to the effect that the perpetrator has sexually assaulted other women. She is even more uncertain as to whether she should inform the police and press charges or not. She wants justice and wants to stop the perpetrator from assaulting other women, but she is fearful that if she presses charges she will be further victimized in a variety of ways: (a) by her family and partner blaming her for what has happened, (b) by the neighborhood viewing her in a more negative light, (c) by having to testify to the details of the assault and having to face the perpetrator and his attorney in court, and (d) by living with the fear that if she presses charges the perpetrator will make life difficult for her in some way. As a social worker, how would you proceed?

Case Example 3:
Ken Natzke is 81 years old and is hospitalized for a few days for a broken leg. He lives in a small house that he has lived in all his life. His wife died 16 years ago, and his two married sons live a few hundred miles away in another city. The sons meet with you (a hospital social worker) and state that they are worried about their father returning home. The house has no running water, is filthy, and is infested with cockroaches. The sons indicate that they have spoken with their dad about their concerns, but he has refused to go to a nursing home. You discuss the case with Mr. Natzke's doctor and discover that Mr. Natzke also has emphysema. His doctor is in favor of a nursing home placement. You then meet with Mr. Natzke. He appears rational but seems to have little physical energy. You mention the concerns raised by his sons. Mr. Natzke informs you that he has thought about moving to a nursing home and has even visited a few. He states that he has decided he will never move to a nursing home. He adds that if he moved to a nursing home he would lose the will to live. He says that he feels he has lived a full life and wants to live his final days in the place where he was born and raised and where he has lived all his life. What would you do?

Case Example 4:
You are a social worker at a nursing home. The nursing home has as yet admitted no one who has AIDS. A 37-year-old male in the final stages of AIDS applies for admission. He has a legal right to be admitted and has no one else to care for him. You accept his admission and inform the nursing staff. The staff verbalizes very few questions at the meeting. However, three days later a representative of the nursing staff informs you that if the person with AIDS is admitted, nearly half of the staff will take a leave of absence or resign. What do you do?

Competencies/Practice Behaviors Exercise 15.3
Role Play—Handling Medical Social Work Cases

Focus Competencies or Practice Behaviors:
- EP 2.1.1b   Practice personal reflection and self-correction to assure continual professional development
- EP 2.1.2a   Recognize and manage personal values in a way that allows professional values to guide practice
- EP 2.1.2b   Make ethical decisions by applying standards of the National Association of Social Workers Code of Ethics and, as applicable, of the International Federation of Social Workers/International Association of Schools of Social Work Ethics in Social Work, Statement of Principles
- EP 2.1.2d   Apply strategies of ethical reasoning to arrive at principled decisions
- EP 2.1.3c   Demonstrate effective oral and written communication in working with individuals, families, groups, organizations, communities, and colleagues
- EP 2.1.4c   Recognize and communicate their understanding of the importance of difference in shaping life experiences
- EP 2.1.7a   Utilize conceptual frameworks to guide the processes of assessment, intervention, and evaluation
- EP 2.1.10a   Substantively and affectively prepare for action with individuals, families, groups, organizations, and communities

A. Brief Description
This exercise is designed to give you simulated experience in medical social work cases and to help you examine some value issues in health care.

B. Objectives
You will:
1. Learn more about medical social work.
2. Experience value issues in health care.
3. Practice your oral communication and critical thinking skills.

C. Procedure
1. Write a paper discussing how you would handle the following vignette.

> **Vignette:**
> Jim Trier, a 14-year-old, is rushed from his high school to the hospital at which Savannah is a social worker. Jim is discovered to have a severe kidney dysfunction and is in need of dialysis. Without dialysis he will die. Jim and his parents belong to a fundamental religious group that is strongly opposed to medical treatment. The parents state that if their son dies, then it is God's will and no one should interfere. The High Priestess of their religious group, Quinella, is also there and is clearly opposed to this medical "interference" with God's will. Jim states, rather passively, that he must abide by his parents' decision.

2. Separate the class into groups of five. One student will assume the role of Jim, one will represent the social worker, Savannah. Two students will portray Jim's parents, Mr. and Mrs. Trier, and one student will be Quinella, the High Priestess.
3. Proceed with the role play for 20 minutes.
4. Bring the class back together to discuss the problems and their thoughts about this role play.

Chapter 15 Competencies/Practice Behaviors Exercises Assessment:

Name: _____ Date: _____
Supervisor's Name: _____

Focus Competencies/Practice Behaviors:
- EP 2.1.1b   Practice personal reflection and self-correction to assure continual professional development
- EP 2.1.2a   Recognize and manage personal values in a way that allows professional values to guide practice
- EP 2.1.2b   Make ethical decisions by applying standards of the National Association of Social Workers Code of Ethics and, as applicable, of the International Federation of Social Workers/International Association of Schools of Social Work Ethics in Social Work, Statement of Principles
- EP 2.1.2d   Apply strategies of ethical reasoning to arrive at principled decisions
- EP 2.1.3c   Demonstrate effective oral and written communication in working with individuals, families, groups, organizations, communities, and colleagues
- EP 2.1.4c   Recognize and communicate their understanding of the importance of difference in shaping life experiences
- EP 2.1.4b   Gain sufficient self-awareness to eliminate the influence of personal biases and values in working with diverse groups
- EP 2.1.5a   Understand forms and mechanisms of oppression and discrimination
- EP 2.1.7a   Utilize conceptual frameworks to guide the processes of assessment, intervention, and evaluation
- EP 2.1.7b   Critique and apply knowledge to understand person and environment
- EP 2.1.10a Substantively and affectively prepare for action with individuals, families, groups, organizations, and communities

Instructions:
A. Evaluate your work or your partner's work in the Focus Competencies/Practice Behaviors by completing the Competencies/Practice Behaviors Assessment form below
B. What other Competencies/Practice Behaviors did you use to complete these Exercises? Be sure to record them in your assessments

1.	I have attained this competency/practice behavior (in the range of 81 to 100%)
2.	I have largely attained this competency/practice behavior (in the range of 61 to 80%)
3.	I have partially attained this competency/practice behavior (in the range of 41 to 60%)
4.	I have made a little progress in attaining this competency/practice behavior (in the range of 21 to 40%)
5.	I have made almost no progress in attaining this competency/practice behavior (in the range of 0 to 20%)

EPAS 2008 Core Competencies & Core Practice Behaviors	Student Self Assessment						Evaluator Feedback
Student and Evaluator Assessment Scale and Comments	0	1	2	3	4	5	Agree/Disagree/Comments
EP 2.1.1 Identify as a Professional Social Worker and Conduct Oneself Accordingly:							
a. Advocate for client access to the services of social work							
b. Practice personal reflection and self-correction to assure continual professional development							
c. Attend to professional roles and boundaries							
d. Demonstrate professional demeanor in behavior, appearance, and communication							
e. Engage in career-long learning							
f. Use supervision and consultation							

EP 2.1.2 Apply Social Work Ethical Principles to Guide Professional Practice:							
a.	Recognize and manage personal values in a way that allows professional values to guide practice						
b.	Make ethical decisions by applying NASW Code of Ethics and, as applicable, of the IFSW/IASSW Ethics in Social Work, Statement of Principles						
c.	Tolerate ambiguity in resolving ethical conflicts						
d.	Apply strategies of ethical reasoning to arrive at principled decisions						
EP 2.1.3 Apply Critical Thinking to Inform and Communicate Professional Judgments:							
a.	Distinguish, appraise, and integrate multiple sources of knowledge, including research-based knowledge and practice wisdom						
b.	Analyze models of assessment, prevention, intervention, and evaluation						
c.	Demonstrate effective oral and written communication in working with individuals, families, groups, organizations, communities, and colleagues						
EP 2.1.4 Engage Diversity and Difference in Practice:							
a.	Recognize the extent to which a culture's structures and values may oppress, marginalize, alienate, or create or enhance privilege and power						
b.	Gain sufficient self-awareness to eliminate the influence of personal biases and values in working with diverse groups						
c.	Recognize and communicate their understanding of the importance of difference in shaping life experiences						
d.	View themselves as learners and engage those with whom they work as informants						
EP 2.1.5 Advance Human Rights and Social and Economic Justice:							
a.	Understand forms and mechanisms of oppression and discrimination						
b.	Advocate for human rights and social and economic justice						
c.	Engage in practices that advance social and economic justice						
EP 2.1.6 Engage in Research-Informed Practice and Practice-Informed Research:							
a.	Use practice experience to inform scientific inquiry						
b.	Use research evidence to inform practice						
EP 2.1.7 Apply Knowledge of Human Behavior and the Social Environment:							
a.	Utilize conceptual frameworks to guide the processes of assessment, intervention, and evaluation						
b.	Critique and apply knowledge to understand person and environment						
EP 2.1.8 Engage in Policy Practice to Advance Social and Economic Well-Being and to Deliver Effective Social Work Services:							
a.	Analyze, formulate, and advocate for policies that advance social well-being						
b.	Collaborate with colleagues and clients for effective policy action						

EP 2.1.9 Respond to Contexts that Shape Practice:							
a.	Continuously discover, appraise, and attend to changing locales, populations, scientific and technological developments, and emerging societal trends to provide relevant services						
b.	Provide leadership in promoting sustainable changes in service delivery and practice to improve the quality of social services						
EP 2.1.10 Engage, Assess, Intervene, and Evaluate with Individuals, Families, Groups, Organizations and Communities:							
a.	Substantively and affectively prepare for action with individuals, families, groups, organizations, and communities						
b.	Use empathy and other interpersonal skills						
c.	Develop a mutually agreed-on focus of work and desired outcomes						
d.	Collect, organize, and interpret client data						
e.	Assess client strengths and limitations						
f.	Develop mutually agreed-on intervention goals and objectives						
g.	Select appropriate intervention strategies						
h.	Initiate actions to achieve organizational goals						
i.	Implement prevention interventions that enhance client capacities						
j.	Help clients resolve problems						
k.	Negotiate, mediate, and advocate for clients						
l.	Facilitate transitions and endings						
m.	Critically analyze, monitor, and evaluate interventions						

Chapter 16: Physical and Mental Disabilities and Rehabilitation

Competencies/Practice Behaviors Exercise 16.1
Experiencing a Disability

Focus Competencies or Practice Behaviors:
- EP 2.1.1b Practice personal reflection and self-correction to assure continual professional development
- EP 2.1.3a Distinguish, appraise, and integrate multiple sources of knowledge, including research-based knowledge and practice wisdom
- EP 2.1.4a Recognize the extent to which a culture's structures and values may oppress, marginalize, alienate, or create or enhance privilege and power
- EP 2.1.4b Gain sufficient self-awareness to eliminate the influence of personal biases and values in working with diverse groups
- EP 2.1.4c Recognize and communicate their understanding of the importance of difference in shaping life experiences
- EP 2.1.5a Understand forms and mechanisms of oppression and discrimination

A. Brief Description
This exercise is designed to increase your awareness of what it is like to have a disability.

B. Objectives
You will:
1. Practice your writing skills.
2. Be more aware of the lives of people with disabilities.

C. Procedure
1. Choose a disability from a list provided by the instructor. You are to simulate as closely as possible what a person with that disability experiences. This simulation should be carried on for a specific but limited period of time (perhaps one day). Examples of disabilities that can be readily simulated include confinement to a wheelchair, blindness (a blindfold is sufficient), hearing disability (ear protectors or cotton in the ears), arthritic conditions (thick gloves on the hands), and missing limbs.
2. Write a paper sharing your experiences, such as how you felt after spending a day simulating this disability, how people treated you, and how this affected your usual routines.

Competencies/Practice Behaviors Exercise 16.2
Role Play—Communicating While Blindfolded

Focus Competencies or Practice Behaviors:
- EP 2.1.1b Practice personal reflection and self-correction to assure continual professional development
- EP 2.1.3a Distinguish, appraise, and integrate multiple sources of knowledge, including research-based knowledge and practice wisdom

- EP 2.1.3c Demonstrate effective oral and written communication in working with individuals, families, groups, organizations, communities, and colleagues
- EP 2.1.4b Gain sufficient self-awareness to eliminate the influence of personal biases and values in working with diverse groups
- EP 2.1.4c Recognize and communicate their understanding of the importance of difference in shaping life experiences
- EP 2.1.7a Utilize conceptual frameworks to guide the processes of assessment, intervention, and evaluation
- EP 2.1.7b Critique and apply knowledge to understand person and environment

A. Brief Description
You should understand how communication is affected when the sense of sight cannot be used.

B. Objectives
You will:
1. Practice your communication skills.
2. Be aware of your sense of sight.

C. Procedure
1. Choose a few classmates or friends to spend 10-15 minutes discussing a controversial topic (for example, whether persons with a cognitive disability who marry should be urged to consider sterilization). All participants will be blindfolded and then should discuss the chosen topic for 10 to 15 minutes.
2. At the end of 10 or 15 minutes, stop the discussion and remove your blindfolds, and form a large circle to discuss the following questions:
    a. How did it feel with the blindfolds on?
    b. How did not being able to see affect the communication?
    c. Did not being able to see interfere with being able to concentrate on what was being said?
    d. Was it difficult hearing what was said?
    e. Do you think you gestured more or less than you usually do?
    f. During this exercise, did you become aware of anything you had not noticed before?
    g. Does not being able to see the people you are talking to substantially hamper communication? If yes, in what ways?
3. Write a paper describing:
    a. The topic of discussion that was chosen.
    b. How you felt while blindfolded during this discussion.
    c. Some of the comments made by the other participants in this exercise during the discussion phase following the exercise.
    d. Whether you felt this exercise was of value.

Chapter 16 Competencies/Practice Behaviors Exercises Assessment:

Name: _____ Date: _____
Supervisor's Name: _____

Focus Competencies/Practice Behaviors:
- EP 2.1.1b   Practice personal reflection and self-correction to assure continual professional development
- EP 2.1.3a   Distinguish, appraise, and integrate multiple sources of knowledge, including research-based knowledge and practice wisdom
- EP 2.1.3c   Demonstrate effective oral and written communication in working with individuals, families, groups, organizations, communities, and colleagues
- EP 2.1.4a   Recognize the extent to which a culture's structures and values may oppress, marginalize, alienate, or create or enhance privilege and power
- EP 2.1.4b   Gain sufficient self-awareness to eliminate the influence of personal biases and values in working with diverse groups
- EP 2.1.4c   Recognize and communicate their understanding of the importance of difference in shaping life experiences
- EP 2.1.5a   Understand forms and mechanisms of oppression and discrimination
- EP 2.1.7a   Utilize conceptual frameworks to guide the processes of assessment, intervention, and evaluation
- EP 2.1.7b   Critique and apply knowledge to understand person and environment

Instructions:
A.   Evaluate your work or your partner's work in the Focus Competencies/Practice Behaviors by completing the Competencies/Practice Behaviors Assessment form below
B.   What other Competencies/Practice Behaviors did you use to complete these Exercises? Be sure to record them in your assessments

1.	I have attained this competency/practice behavior (in the range of 81 to 100%)
2.	I have largely attained this competency/practice behavior (in the range of 61 to 80%)
3.	I have partially attained this competency/practice behavior (in the range of 41 to 60%)
4.	I have made a little progress in attaining this competency/practice behavior (in the range of 21 to 40%)
5.	I have made almost no progress in attaining this competency/practice behavior (in the range of 0 to 20%)

EPAS 2008 Core Competencies & Core Practice Behaviors			Student Self Assessment					Evaluator Feedback
Student and Evaluator Assessment Scale and Comments		0	1	2	3	4	5	Agree/Disagree/Comments
EP 2.1.1 Identify as a Professional Social Worker and Conduct Oneself Accordingly:								
a.	Advocate for client access to the services of social work							
b.	Practice personal reflection and self-correction to assure continual professional development							
c.	Attend to professional roles and boundaries							
d.	Demonstrate professional demeanor in behavior, appearance, and communication							
e.	Engage in career-long learning							
f.	Use supervision and consultation							

EP 2.1.2 Apply Social Work Ethical Principles to Guide Professional Practice:							
a.	Recognize and manage personal values in a way that allows professional values to guide practice						
b.	Make ethical decisions by applying NASW Code of Ethics and, as applicable, of the IFSW/IASSW Ethics in Social Work, Statement of Principles						
c.	Tolerate ambiguity in resolving ethical conflicts						
d.	Apply strategies of ethical reasoning to arrive at principled decisions						
EP 2.1.3 Apply Critical Thinking to Inform and Communicate Professional Judgments:							
a.	Distinguish, appraise, and integrate multiple sources of knowledge, including research-based knowledge and practice wisdom						
b.	Analyze models of assessment, prevention, intervention, and evaluation						
c.	Demonstrate effective oral and written communication in working with individuals, families, groups, organizations, communities, and colleagues						
EP 2.1.4 Engage Diversity and Difference in Practice:							
a.	Recognize the extent to which a culture's structures and values may oppress, marginalize, alienate, or create or enhance privilege and power						
b.	Gain sufficient self-awareness to eliminate the influence of personal biases and values in working with diverse groups						
c.	Recognize and communicate their understanding of the importance of difference in shaping life experiences						
d.	View themselves as learners and engage those with whom they work as informants						
EP 2.1.5 Advance Human Rights and Social and Economic Justice:							
a.	Understand forms and mechanisms of oppression and discrimination						
b.	Advocate for human rights and social and economic justice						
c.	Engage in practices that advance social and economic justice						
EP 2.1.6 Engage in Research-Informed Practice and Practice-Informed Research:							
a.	Use practice experience to inform scientific inquiry						
b.	Use research evidence to inform practice						
EP 2.1.7 Apply Knowledge of Human Behavior and the Social Environment:							
a.	Utilize conceptual frameworks to guide the processes of assessment, intervention, and evaluation						
b.	Critique and apply knowledge to understand person and environment						
EP 2.1.8 Engage in Policy Practice to Advance Social and Economic Well-Being and to Deliver Effective Social Work Services:							
a.	Analyze, formulate, and advocate for policies that advance social well-being						
b.	Collaborate with colleagues and clients for effective policy action						

EP 2.1.9 Respond to Contexts that Shape Practice:							
a. Continuously discover, appraise, and attend to changing locales, populations, scientific and technological developments, and emerging societal trends to provide relevant services							
b. Provide leadership in promoting sustainable changes in service delivery and practice to improve the quality of social services							
EP 2.1.10 Engage, Assess, Intervene, and Evaluate with Individuals, Families, Groups, Organizations and Communities:							
a. Substantively and affectively prepare for action with individuals, families, groups, organizations, and communities							
b. Use empathy and other interpersonal skills							
c. Develop a mutually agreed-on focus of work and desired outcomes							
d. Collect, organize, and interpret client data							
e. Assess client strengths and limitations							
f. Develop mutually agreed-on intervention goals and objectives							
g. Select appropriate intervention strategies							
h. Initiate actions to achieve organizational goals							
i. Implement prevention interventions that enhance client capacities							
j. Help clients resolve problems							
k. Negotiate, mediate, and advocate for clients							
l. Facilitate transitions and endings							
m. Critically analyze, monitor, and evaluate interventions							

Chapter 17: Overpopulation, Misuse of the Environment, and Family Planning

Competencies/Practice Behaviors Exercise 17.1
Values Clarification on Overpopulation Issues

Focus Competencies or Practice Behaviors:
- EP 2.1.1b Practice personal reflection and self-correction to assure continual professional development
- EP 2.1.2a Recognize and manage personal values in a way that allows professional values to guide practice
- EP 2.1.2b Make ethical decisions by applying standards of the National Association of Social Workers Code of Ethics and, as applicable, of the International Federation of Social Workers/International Association of Schools of Social Work Ethics in Social Work, Statement of Principles
- EP 2.1.3a Distinguish, appraise, and integrate multiple sources of knowledge, including research-based knowledge and practice wisdom
- EP 2.1.4a Recognize the extent to which a culture's structures and values may oppress, marginalize, alienate, or create or enhance privilege and power
- EP 2.1.4b Gain sufficient self-awareness to eliminate the influence of personal biases and values in working with diverse groups
- EP 2.1.6b Use research evidence to inform practice
- EP 2.1.7a Utilize conceptual frameworks to guide the processes of assessment, intervention, and evaluation
- EP 2.1.7b Critique and apply knowledge to understand person and environment
- EP 2.1.9a Continuously discover, appraise, and attend to changing locales, populations, scientific and technological developments, and emerging societal trends to provide relevant services
- EP 2.1.10a Substantively and affectively prepare for action with individuals, families, groups, organizations, and communities

A. Brief Description
This exercise is designed to inform you about overpopulation issues and to help you clarify your positions and values on these issues.

B. Objectives
You will:
1. Learn more about overpopulation.
2. Become more aware of your personal views about overpopulation.

C. Procedure
1. Complete the following questionnaire.

Overpopulation Issues

1. There are nearly 7 billion people living on this planet. In 65 years the population will double in size unless population control measures are enacted. Do you believe population control measures should be enacted?
    a. Yes
    b. No

2. Specify what you think is the optimum size of the world's population:
    a. Under 6 billion
    b. Around 6 billion
    c. Between 6 and 10 billion
    d. Over 10 billion
    e. Over 20 billion

3. What measures do you think should be used to control the size of the world's population? Check all those that you think should be used.
    a. Birth control devices
    b. Abortion by choice
    c. Involuntary abortions for those women having three or more live children
    d. Voluntary sterilization
    e. Involuntary sterilization for those women having three or more live children
    f. None of the above

4. Do you believe everyone needs to focus on preserving and conserving resources?
    a. Yes
    b. No

5. Are you willing to conserve resources by buying only compact, energy-efficient cars?
    a. Yes
    b. No

6. Do you believe that abortion is an essential population-control technique? (In some countries, the number of abortions is approaching the number of live births.)
    a. Yes
    b. No

7. Do you believe Medicaid funds should be used to enable lower-income women who desire an abortion to obtain an abortion?
    a. Yes
    b. No

8. Do you believe the United States should require foreign countries to establish effective population-control programs before giving them foreign aid?
    a. Yes
    b. No

9. Do you believe undocumented immigrants are primarily an asset to the United States or a social problem?
    a. Asset
    b. Social problem

> 10. Do you believe persons who test positive for the AIDS virus ought to be allowed to immigrate to the United States?
>   a. Yes
>   b. No
>
> 11. Should the number of people who are allowed to immigrate annually to the United States be increased or decreased?
>   a. Increased
>   b. Decreased
>
> 12. Due to the dangers of radioactive leaks from nuclear power plants, do you believe the United States should ban future construction of nuclear power plants?
>   a. Yes
>   b. No
>
> 13. Do you believe RU-486 (a pill that induces abortion early in pregnancy) should be used in the United States?
>   a. Yes
>   b. No
>
> 14. Do you believe Planned Parenthood clinics should be physically located in high schools to provide greater access by students to birth control information and contraceptives?
>   a. Yes
>   b. No

2. The instructor will anonymously record the answers to this questionnaire on the board. A discussion will then begin regarding these answers, and how you feel about them.

Competencies/Practice Behaviors Exercise 17.2
Saving Our Planet

Focus Competencies or Practice Behaviors:
- EP 2.1.1b   Practice personal reflection and self-correction to assure continual professional development
- EP 2.1.2a   Recognize and manage personal values in a way that allows professional values to guide practice
- EP 2.1.3a   Distinguish, appraise, and integrate multiple sources of knowledge, including research-based knowledge and practice wisdom
- EP 2.1.4a   Recognize the extent to which a culture's structures and values may oppress, marginalize, alienate, or create or enhance privilege and power
- EP 2.1.6a   Use practice experience to inform scientific inquiry
- EP 2.1.7a   Utilize conceptual frameworks to guide the processes of assessment, intervention, and evaluation
- EP 2.1.7b   Critique and apply knowledge to understand person and environment
- EP 2.1.8a   Analyze, formulate, and advocate for policies that advance social well-being

- EP 2.1.9a Continuously discover, appraise, and attend to changing locales, populations, scientific and technological developments, and emerging societal trends to provide relevant services
- EP 2.1.10a Substantively and affectively prepare for action with individuals, families, groups, organizations, and communities

A. Brief Description
This exercise is designed to help inform you of what you can do to preserve our environment.

B. Objectives
You will:
1. Learn more about saving our planet.
2. Become more aware of your personal views about this issue.

C. Procedure
1. Read the corresponding chapter in the text. Fill out this questionnaire and hand in to the instructor.

Saving Our Planet

By everyone taking small steps, major improvements will occur in our environment. The following are simple things you can do to help the earth. Please indicate in responses (a) "Yes" or (b) "No" whether you are willing to take the indicated action. Then indicate in responses (c) "Currently doing" or (d) "Currently not doing" whether you are presently taking the indicated action. Be honest!

1. Use mugs instead of paper cups
   a. Yes   c. Currently doing
   b. No   d. Currently not doing

2. Use washable cotton towels instead of paper towels
   a. Yes   c. Currently doing
   b. No   d. Currently not doing

3. Use cloth napkins instead of paper napkins
   a. Yes   c. Currently doing
   b. No   d. Currently not doing

4. Use both sides of sheets of paper when notetaking
   a. Yes   c. Currently doing
   b. No   d. Currently not doing

5. When you shop, have a mind-set in which you seek to buy products that are recyclable rather than disposable
   a. Yes   c. Currently doing
   b. No   d. Currently not doing

6. Reduce use of Styrofoam cups, which tend to be non-biodegradable
   a. Yes   c. Currently doing
   b. No   d. Currently not doing

7. Take showers of less than five minutes instead of long showers or baths
   a. Yes
   b. No
   c. Currently doing
   d. Currently not doing

8. Not run water continuously when brushing your teeth
   a. Yes
   b. No
   c. Currently doing
   d. Currently not doing

9. Conserve water by placing a brick or a jug of water in the water container of your toilet
   a. Yes
   b. No
   c. Currently doing
   d. Currently not doing

10. Buy beverages in returnable containers and then return them
    a. Yes
    b. No
    c. Currently doing
    d. Currently not doing

11. Reduce the amount of heat that you use in winter by such actions as turning down the thermostat at night or wearing a sweater instead of turning up the heat
    a. Yes
    b. No
    c. Currently doing
    d. Currently not doing

12. Open blinds during day for heat from sun during cold weather, and close at night to conserve heat
    a. Yes
    b. No
    c. Currently doing
    d. Currently not doing

13. Close blinds during the day in hot weather to reduce air conditioning costs
    a. Yes
    b. No
    c. Currently doing
    d. Currently not doing

14. Buy and use cars that are fuel efficient
    a. Yes
    b. No
    c. Currently doing
    d. Currently not doing

15. Reduce food wastes, which are major contributors to garbage
    a. Yes
    b. No
    c. Currently doing
    d. Currently not doing

16. When you shop, have a mind-set in which you try to buy products that are made out of recycled paper or other recycled products
    a. Yes
    b. No
    c. Currently doing
    d. Currently not doing

17. Have a mind-set in which you try not to litter
    a. Yes
    b. No
    c. Currently doing
    d. Currently not doing

18. Have a mind-set in which you try to use soap detergents that are low in phosphate
    a. Yes
    b. No
    c. Currently doing
    d. Currently not doing

> 19. Have a mind-set in which you try to avoid purchasing products made from endangered species—such as ivory, tortoise shells, and reptile shells
>   a. Yes   c. Currently doing
>   b. No   d. Currently not doing
>
> 20. Buy eggs in paperboard cartons instead of plastic foam cartons (which tend to be non-biodegradable)
>   a. Yes   c. Currently doing
>   b. No   d. Currently not doing
>
> 21. Have a mind-set in which you try to purchase meat, poultry, and other products that are wrapped in paper rather than plastic
>   a. Yes   c. Currently doing
>   b. No   d. Currently not doing
>
> 22. Have a mind-set in which you are careful not to place toxic waste products into garbage containers
>   a. Yes   c. Currently doing
>   b. No   d. Currently not doing

2. The instructor will tabulate the responses and write these on the board, while preserving anonymity.

Competencies/Practice Behaviors Exercise 17.3
Role Play—Values Clarification about Overpopulation and Preserving the Environment

Focus Competencies or Practice Behaviors:
- EP 2.1.1b   Practice personal reflection and self-correction to assure continual professional development
- EP 2.1.3a   Distinguish, appraise, and integrate multiple sources of knowledge, including research-based knowledge and practice wisdom
- EP 2.1.3b   Analyze models of assessment, prevention, intervention, and evaluation
- EP 2.1.3c   Demonstrate effective oral and written communication in working with individuals, families, groups, organizations, communities, and colleagues
- EP 2.1.4a   Recognize the extent to which a culture's structures and values may oppress, marginalize, alienate, or create or enhance privilege and power
- EP 2.1.6a   Use practice experience to inform scientific inquiry
- EP 2.1.7a   Utilize conceptual frameworks to guide the processes of assessment, intervention, and evaluation
- EP 2.1.9a   Continuously discover, appraise, and attend to changing locales, populations, scientific and technological developments, and emerging societal trends to provide relevant services
- EP 2.1.10a   Substantively and affectively prepare for action with individuals, families, groups, organizations, and communities

A. Brief Description
   This role play is designed to help you clarify your values concerning overpopulation and preserving the environment.

B. Objectives
   You will:
   1. Become more aware of your personal values.
   2. Learn more about overpopulation and preserving the environment.

C. Procedure
   1. Read the problems described in this chapter concerning the dangers of overpopulation and the dangers in using nuclear energy.
   2. Divide the class into groups of six, and assign each group one of the following issues.
   3. Three of the students with argue one side of the issue and the other three will argue the opposite side of it.
      a. Should a constitutional amendment be passed prohibiting abortions?
      b. Should Planned Parenthood clinics be physically located in high schools to provide greater access by students to birth control information and contraceptives?
      c. Should the United States establish for our country a population control policy in which every adult who parents three or more children is required to be sterilized?
      d. Should the use of nuclear power plants in this country be prohibited?
      e. If a male contraceptive pill was approved for use in this country, do you believe it would be as widely used by men as the female contraceptive pill is being used by women? Present your reasons.
   4. The groups will then discuss how they felt about these issues, and how difficult it was to argue for or against something that was contrary to their own personal views.

Chapter 17 Competencies/Practice Behaviors Exercises Assessment:

Name: _____ **Date:** _____
Supervisor's Name: _____

Focus Competencies/Practice Behaviors:
- EP 2.1.1b   Practice personal reflection and self-correction to assure continual professional development
- EP 2.1.2a   Recognize and manage personal values in a way that allows professional values to guide practice
- EP 2.1.2b   Make ethical decisions by applying standards of the National Association of Social Workers Code of Ethics and, as applicable, of the International Federation of Social Workers/International Association of Schools of Social Work Ethics in Social Work, Statement of Principles
- EP 2.1.3a   Distinguish, appraise, and integrate multiple sources of knowledge, including research-based knowledge and practice wisdom
- EP 2.1.3b   Analyze models of assessment, prevention, intervention, and evaluation
- EP 2.1.3c   Demonstrate effective oral and written communication in working with individuals, families, groups, organizations, communities, and colleagues
- EP 2.1.4a   Recognize the extent to which a culture's structures and values may oppress, marginalize, alienate, or create or enhance privilege and power
- EP 2.1.4b   Gain sufficient self-awareness to eliminate the influence of personal biases and values in working with diverse groups
- EP 2.1.6a   Use practice experience to inform scientific inquiry
- EP 2.1.6b   Use research evidence to inform practice
- EP 2.1.7a   Utilize conceptual frameworks to guide the processes of assessment, intervention, and evaluation
- EP 2.1.7b   Critique and apply knowledge to understand person and environment
- EP 2.1.8a   Analyze, formulate, and advocate for policies that advance social well-being
- EP 2.1.9a   Continuously discover, appraise, and attend to changing locales, populations, scientific and technological developments, and emerging societal trends to provide relevant services
- EP 2.1.10a   Substantively and affectively prepare for action with individuals, families, groups, organizations, and communities

Instructions:
A.   Evaluate your work or your partner's work in the Focus Competencies/Practice Behaviors by completing the Competencies/Practice Behaviors Assessment form below
B.   What other Competencies/Practice Behaviors did you use to complete these Exercises? Be sure to record them in your assessments

1.	I have attained this competency/practice behavior (in the range of 81 to 100%)
2.	I have largely attained this competency/practice behavior (in the range of 61 to 80%)
3.	I have partially attained this competency/practice behavior (in the range of 41 to 60%)
4.	I have made a little progress in attaining this competency/practice behavior (in the range of 21 to 40%)
5.	I have made almost no progress in attaining this competency/practice behavior (in the range of 0 to 20%)

EPAS 2008 Core Competencies & Core Practice Behaviors	Student Self Assessment						Evaluator Feedback
Student and Evaluator Assessment Scale and Comments	0	1	2	3	4	5	Agree/Disagree/Comments
EP 2.1.1 Identify as a Professional Social Worker and Conduct Oneself Accordingly:							
a. Advocate for client access to the services of social work							
b. Practice personal reflection and self-correction to assure continual professional development							
c. Attend to professional roles and boundaries							
d. Demonstrate professional demeanor in behavior, appearance, and communication							
e. Engage in career-long learning							
f. Use supervision and consultation							
EP 2.1.2 Apply Social Work Ethical Principles to Guide Professional Practice:							
a. Recognize and manage personal values in a way that allows professional values to guide practice							
b. Make ethical decisions by applying NASW Code of Ethics and, as applicable, of the IFSW/IASSW Ethics in Social Work, Statement of Principles							
c. Tolerate ambiguity in resolving ethical conflicts							
d. Apply strategies of ethical reasoning to arrive at principled decisions							
EP 2.1.3 Apply Critical Thinking to Inform and Communicate Professional Judgments:							
a. Distinguish, appraise, and integrate multiple sources of knowledge, including research-based knowledge and practice wisdom							
b. Analyze models of assessment, prevention, intervention, and evaluation							
c. Demonstrate effective oral and written communication in working with individuals, families, groups, organizations, communities, and colleagues							
EP 2.1.4 Engage Diversity and Difference in Practice:							
a. Recognize the extent to which a culture's structures and values may oppress, marginalize, alienate, or create or enhance privilege and power							
b. Gain sufficient self-awareness to eliminate the influence of personal biases and values in working with diverse groups							
c. Recognize and communicate their understanding of the importance of difference in shaping life experiences							
d. View themselves as learners and engage those with whom they work as informants							
EP 2.1.5 Advance Human Rights and Social and Economic Justice:							
a. Understand forms and mechanisms of oppression and discrimination							
b. Advocate for human rights and social and economic justice							
c. Engage in practices that advance social and economic justice							
EP 2.1.6 Engage in Research-Informed Practice and Practice-Informed Research:							
a. Use practice experience to inform scientific inquiry							
b. Use research evidence to inform practice							

EP 2.1.7 Apply Knowledge of Human Behavior and the Social Environment:						
a.	Utilize conceptual frameworks to guide the processes of assessment, intervention, and evaluation					
b.	Critique and apply knowledge to understand person and environment					
EP 2.1.8 Engage in Policy Practice to Advance Social and Economic Well-Being and to Deliver Effective Social Work Services:						
a.	Analyze, formulate, and advocate for policies that advance social well-being					
b.	Collaborate with colleagues and clients for effective policy action					
EP 2.1.9 Respond to Contexts that Shape Practice:						
a.	Continuously discover, appraise, and attend to changing locales, populations, scientific and technological developments, and emerging societal trends to provide relevant services					
b.	Provide leadership in promoting sustainable changes in service delivery and practice to improve the quality of social services					
EP 2.1.10 Engage, Assess, Intervene, and Evaluate with Individuals, Families, Groups, Organizations and Communities:						
a.	Substantively and affectively prepare for action with individuals, families, groups, organizations, and communities					
b.	Use empathy and other interpersonal skills					
c.	Develop a mutually agreed-on focus of work and desired outcomes					
d.	Collect, organize, and interpret client data					
e.	Assess client strengths and limitations					
f.	Develop mutually agreed-on intervention goals and objectives					
g.	Select appropriate intervention strategies					
h.	Initiate actions to achieve organizational goals					
i.	Implement prevention interventions that enhance client capacities					
j.	Help clients resolve problems					
k.	Negotiate, mediate, and advocate for clients					
l.	Facilitate transitions and endings					
m.	Critically analyze, monitor, and evaluate interventions					

CPSIA information can be obtained
at www.ICGtesting.com
Printed in the USA
FFOW03n0047040815
15695FF